Working
with
Metal

Working with Metal

Pamela Tubby

Thomas Y. Crowell, Publishers
Established 1834
New York

This book was created, designed and produced by
Reference International, 21, Soho Square, London,
in association with Martensson Books, London.

Executive editor	Wendy Martensson
Editor	David Parker
Design	Julian Holland
Photography	Chris Overton
	Richard Mummery
Photo research	Alice Baker
Illustrations	Don Parry

ISBN 0–690–01816–9
LC 78–65662

Published in the USA 1979 by
Thomas Y. Crowell
New York, N.Y.

Printed in the United States

Contents

	Introduction	7
Chapter one	Introduction to metals	8
Chapter two	The workshop	20
Chapter three	Basic tools and working techniques	30
Chapter four	Fastening metals together	62
Chapter five	Soldering	74
Chapter six	Sheet metalwork	82
Chapter seven	Wrought iron	92
Chapter eight	Beaten metalwork	104
Chapter nine	Finishing metal	120
Chapter ten	Projects	134
	Comparative tables	152
	Index	154

Introduction

Between a school workshop and an evening class, few people have much opportunity to learn about metalcraft. Working with Metal fills this gap. It is aimed at the complete beginner who knows little or nothing about metalwork. If you have never before picked up a piece of metal with the intention of shaping it, or if you would like to make something in metal but you find jewelry making not quite what you want and blacksmithing too daunting, then this is the book for you. It introduces the world of metalworking in a way that brings it well within the scope of the amateur home craftsman. Basic processes are introduced in a clear and simple way so that you will have a number of different techniques at your fingertips.

The book begins with an introduction to the metals and their properties, explains which metals are best to work with and why, and tells you how to go about buying ferrous and non-ferrous metals.

The most basic tools for metalworking often differ from the more familiar tools used for woodworking and general handyman and craftwork. Working with Metal illustrates each tool, explains its different uses and gives necessary specifications so that even if you have never seen one before, you can go into a shop and buy the best tool for each job without having to learn through expensive mistakes.

Working with Metal will introduce you to the various ways in which you can cut, shape and join metals in a home workshop, explaining the procedure, introducing the tools required and showing you how to avoid and correct mistakes so that not only will you be able to perform each operation correctly, but you will be equipped to judge which technique is best for each job.

The book ends with a number of very simple projects using many of the techniques introduced in the book. Detailed instructions are given for making each one, and there are also many suggestions to help you plan your own projects.

Working with Metal will be a useful addition to the bookshelves of many other craftworkers too. If you would like to experiment with using metals in combination with other materials, you will find that this book gives you all the information you need to cut and shape the metal to your requirements. Model-makers, whatever their speciality, and home handymen will also find this book useful on many occasions.

Working with Metal is an introduction and stepping stone into the wider world of working with that most ancient and engrossing of materials—metal.

CHAPTER ONE

Introduction to metals

HISTORY OF METALWORKING

Metals are among nature's most common elements but only gold, silver, copper and platinum are found in a pure state. Most other metals are mined as ore—a mixture of rock, soil, metal and various chemical elements.

These metals are refined by melting ore and running off the molten metal. Some, tin for example, can be extracted quite easily by crushing and washing the ore. Other metals, for example aluminum, can only be extracted by a complicated industrial process.

Copper

Copper is one of the earliest metals known. There are records of mines on Sinai as far back as 4700 BC, and later there were mines on Cyprus and many places around the Mediterranean. The earliest tools and implements for which traces have been found were made of copper. It is malleable and very easy to work and resists corrosion well. Today copper is most highly prized for its qualities as a conductor of electricity.

Pure copper is a very soft metal, but mixed with tin it forms the much harder and stronger alloy, bronze. The development of bronze meant that really hard tools and arms could be made for the first time.

Bronze was first made around 3500 BC in Asia Minor and the method of making the alloy soon became known around the Mediterranean. The Phoenicians exported tin from Spain and Britain and developed a bronze trade around the world. This alloy was so important that it gave its name to an era—the Bronze Age.

Around 1000 BC, iron began to replace bronze as the metal used for tools and weapons. The most ancient piece of iron known is a blade found in an Egyptian pyramid. It is quite possible that iron was discovered and the process then forgotten many times in pre-history, because unlike copper, which is very resistant to corrosion, iron rusts and disintegrates.

In early iron working, the ore was heated in a charcoal fire until the molten metal ran out. The white hot metal was then hammered vigorously to force out slag, stone and sand. Very high quality wrought iron was produced in this way. Some of the finest ironwork ever made was produced during the Middle Ages. Beautiful, intricate wrought ironwork and finely crafted arms and armor were all made by simple, almost primitive processes. The basic processes for working iron have not changed much since then. Vast modern industrial machinery is often only duplicating on a large scale the action of a man's arm.

Many basic metalworking techniques and processes were developed early in history. The ancient Egyptians were the first to use riveting, and the Greeks perfected many techniques including chasing, embossing and enameling. They also did soft soldering with tin and hard soldering using copper alloys. The Greeks knew of steel and mercury which they called quicksilver and the Romans used lead sheet for water pipes. Their name for lead was "plumbum," the source of our own word plumber, a worker in lead.

New metals continued to be discovered or refined until the early years of this century. Bismuth and antimony were not known until the Middle Ages; nickel, tungsten, and titanium until the eighteenth century and magnesium, bauxite and vanadium until the nineteenth century.

In this century many processes have been refined and new ones developed, for example chrome plating, new welding methods, automatic and computor controlled processes and the development of strong lightweight alloys for the aerospace industry—duralumin and alloys using titanium, beryllium and molybdenum.

The first step in beginning to work with a new material is to learn about some of the qualities of that material. The better you understand a material, the more successful will be your work with it. The following pages will give you a brief and general introduction to metals. First, the properties of metal, second, some of the common metalworking processes and third, a description of the metals themselves.

Each metal has many physical and chemical properties which determine its uses and affect the way in which it is worked. Metals are described by their properties and each metal is selected for a particular job because of the properties which make it the best material for that job. When you are planning any metalworking project you should first investigate the properties of the various metals which you might choose and make your choice so that the properties of the metal are working for you and not against you.

THE PROPERTIES OF METALS

Age hardening
A slow hardening process which occurs in aluminum alloys, especially duralumin, when the metal is left at room temperature. The metal must be re-annealed, that is softened by heating, if it is to be worked after age hardening.

Brittleness
Brittleness causes metal to break without deformation or warning as a result of a sharp blow. Cast iron and heat hardened high carbon steels are very brittle. This property is the opposite of toughness, but hardness and brittleness are often related. Hard metals are more brittle than soft metals.

Color
Used as a means of identification and as a guide in judging heat treatments (see page 60). An important quality in decorative work.

Conductivity
Most metals conduct heat and electricity. Silver, copper and pure aluminum are the best conductors.

Contraction
Most metals expand with heat and contract on cooling. Antimony is an exception. For this reason it is used, alloyed with lead and tin, in type metal to produce clear letters for printing.

Ductility
The property that allows metal to be drawn out thin or deformed without breaking. Ductility often increases with heat. Copper and silver are very ductile. Ductility bears little relation to malleability. Lead, for example, is malleable but not ductile.

Elasticity
The ability of a metal to regain its size and shape after bending, stretching or compressing. The steel used for springs is very elastic.

Fusibility
The ability of a metal to become liquid easily and to join with other metals when it is heated. This property is important in processes like smelting, casting, soldering and welding. Different metals have different melting points. For example, mercury melts well below freezing point, caesium melts at the same temperature as butter, while tungsten melts at 6150°F (3400°C).

Hardness
The resistance a metal offers to being scratched, cut or worn down. The harder a metal is, the less likely it is to change shape under outside pressures. Hardness can be increased by heat treatment or work hardening.

Magnetism
Iron and steel are important magnetic metals. Others—cobalt, nickel and manganese—are only slightly magnetic.

Malleability
Malleability allows a metal to be bent, hammered or rolled without breaking or cracking. Gold is the most malleable metal of all. It can be beaten out to a leaf 1/25000 of an inch thick.

Toughness
The ability of a metal to withstand hard blows or sudden shocks without breaking. This is the opposite of brittleness and one of the most important properties of metals. Toughness decreases with heating, so annealing is necessary to make a tough metal easy to work.

Work hardening
Metals harden when they are hammered or bent. Hardness causes brittleness and so the hardened metal must be annealed to prevent it from cracking during the working process.

METALWORKING PROCESSES

The term "metalworking" covers a wide variety of processes and working techniques. Most of the basic techniques have not changed fundamentally since the Middle Ages and are continued today whether in a small craftsman's workshop or on a massive scale in industry. Some of the processes described—case hardening, welding or extruding for example—are beyond the scope of someone doing metalwork at home, but they are related to the metalwork you will do in your workshop because many of them are used in industry to make the tools and fittings you use at home.

The following is a glossary of some of the most common metalworking processes.

Annealing
Annealing is heating metal to produce its softest working state and allow cold working to continue. The metal must be cooled slowly as the slower the cooling, the softer the metal becomes. You will need to anneal metal often while doing beaten metalwork as metals harden when they are hammered. The procedure for annealing both ferrous and non-ferrous metals, that is metals containing iron or not, is explained on page 61.

Case hardening
This is a method of hardening the outer surface of wrought iron or mild steel by adding carbon to the outside. The hard outer skin of case hardened steel is resistant to wear while the inside is tough. The process is used to produce parts such as screws for machines, hand tools, ball and roller bearings. It is no use if tools need regrinding.

Casting
Casting is the process of making metal shapes by pouring molten metal into prepared molds.

Drawing
Drawing can have two meanings, the best known is the process of pulling ductile metals through holes in a plate to reduce their cross-section. Jewelers often use this technique to produce wire that is not of standard thickness. The metal is drawn through a number of holes, each gradually reducing in size. Drawing is also the name for the industrial process of forming sheet metal into a seamless hollow shape using a punch that forces the metal into the die cavity. The process is similar to pressing.

Extruding
Extruding is an industrial process in which metals are forced through holes to produce bars, sections or tubes. The principle is the same as squeezing a toothpaste tube. The advantage of this process is that complex shapes can be produced in long, uniform pieces. Most extruding is done with the metal hot, but lead, tin and aluminum can be extruded cold.

Forging

Shaping metal by hammering is called forging. This is probably the earliest of all the metalworking processes and is as old as civilization itself. As well as shaping, it improves the quality of the metal and increases its toughness and strength. Usually the metal must be red hot, although some metals and some forging techniques can be worked cold. In traditional hand forging, the blacksmith hammers the red hot metal against different parts of the anvil to achieve a variety of shapes. Industrial processes use huge forging hammers and forging presses to shape metals that must stand up to great stress.

Hardening

Hardening is producing the maximum hardness in carbon steel by heating the metal and then quenching it in water, brine or oil. The process makes the metal brittle and reduces ductility. It is usually followed by tempering. Hardening is done industrially to the sharpened cutting edges of tools. In the home workshop it is used to restore hardness to tools that have become blunt and lost their temper. The process is explained on page 61.

Normalizing

Normalizing refines the structure of metal and relieves the stresses set up by working it. It is used to restore steel to its normal condition after forging or incorrect heat treatment. The metal is heated above the hardening temperature and then cooled in air. The process is similar to annealing.

Spinning

A fast revolving sheet of ductile metal is forced over a wooden or metal former in this process. It is primarily an industrial process, although it can be done on a lathe in a home workshop. A lot of aluminum alloy kitchenware is made in this way. Spinning can be used to produce shapes with contoured sides which are difficult to make in any other way.

Tempering

Tempering reduces the brittleness in steel after it has been hardened. It also increases the toughness. Tempering is done by heating and then cooling the metal, the temperature to which it is heated and the speed of cooling vary according to the type of steel.

Welding

This process is that of permanently joining metal either by hammering at white heat (forge welding) or fusing together with molten metal (oxyacetylene or electric arc welding). It is possible to rent the equipment necessary to do welding at home, or to buy welders which can be powered by a car battery, but this is really a skilled process because of the equipment required and the great heat which is generated. The related processes of soldering and brazing are well within the scope of any home craftsman.

THE METALS

Metals are classed as pure metals and alloys which are mixtures of different metals. Metals are rarely used in a pure state. By alloying them, metals can be changed to suit almost any requirement and it is possible to produce an almost infinite range of alloys with varying properties, suitable for almost any need.

The following is a listing of the metals we commonly encounter, some of which are suited for metalwork at home.

FERROUS METALS

Iron

Iron is the only ferrous metal, but the term is used to include all alloys which contain iron. Iron is the most common metal comprising 5% of the earth's crust but pure iron is difficult to produce and is rarely used. However, by the addition of carbon, iron is changed to steel which is much tougher and is one of the most useful alloys we have.

Cast iron

Cast iron was once used extensively, but now steel, which is much tougher, has taken its place. Cast iron is very hard and brittle. It can be sawn, filed or drilled, but it cannot be bent or forged. It rusts slowly. Cast iron is used for heavy parts of many machines—bases, cylinder blocks—and for piston rings and fireplace grates.

Malleable castings

Cast iron which has been annealed to give increased strength, toughness and elasticity is known as malleable castings. It is used for plumbing fixtures, castings that have to withstand shock or that need further work done on them.

Wrought iron

Made of almost pure iron, wrought iron is malleable and can be shaped and bent hot or cold. It is easy to saw, chisel, file, drill, braze and solder. However, wrought iron is soon attacked by rust and should be protected with paint for outdoor use and for indoor use with wax. It is used for decorative work, such as screens, gates and brackets.

Steel

Steel is an alloy of iron and carbon, and today it is the most important and versatile alloy produced.

Mild steel

This is comparatively soft steel, containing only small quantities of carbon and is therefore also known as low carbon steel. It is easy to work and can be bent, filed, sawn or drilled. Mild steel can also be soldered and brazed. It rusts easily and should be protected with paint or clear lacquer. It is produced in vast quantities for structural work, for cars and tinplate and to make wire, nails, screws, rivets, nuts, bolts and tubes.

Black mild steel

Mild steel covered with a black scale formed by oxidation during hot rolling is known as black mild steel. It bends well cold.

Bright drawn mild steel

This alloy is produced by cleaning black mild steel and then cold rolling it which gives a bright, clean finish. It is stronger but less ductile than black mild steel.

Medium carbon steel

As the carbon content increases, so does the strength and hardness of the steel. Medium carbon steel contains from 0.3% to 0.7% carbon. It is used to make nuts and bolts and vehicle axles.

High carbon steel

High carbon steel contains up to 1.3% carbon. It is hard and brittle, although like all steels it can be tempered. It forges well although not as easily as mild steel. It is not easy to file, saw or machine and it rusts easily.

Cast steel

Cast steel is high carbon steel hardened by heating and quenching after which it can be tempered. When the carbon content is above 0.9% it is called tool steel and is used to make cutting tools such as razor blades, drills, taps, dies and chisels.

High speed steel

Plain carbon steels become soft at temperatures above 572°F (300°C). High speed steel contains tungsten, chromium, vanadium and manganese in varying quantities and combinations which enable it to cut at high speed and keep its hardness when hot. It makes efficient cutting tools.

Stainless steel
The composition varies, but all stainless steels contain at least 12% chromium. Stainless steel is expensive and difficult to work, but it is very tough and can be soldered and brazed. It does not rust and is therefore used for cutlery, kitchenware and furniture frames.

Tinplate
Mild steel sheet covered with a thin protective coating of tin is known as tinplate. The tin is applied either by dipping or electro-plating. The iron center rusts if the tin coating is scratched. Tinplate bends easily and can be soft soldered. It is used for household utensils, guttering, water tanks and pipes.

Galvanized iron
Galvanized iron is mild steel sheet coated with zinc. It is used in much the same way as tinplate.

Terne plate
Mild steel sheet coated with lead or an alloy of tin and lead is called terne plate. It solders easily and holds lubricants well. It is used for radio chassis.

Alloy steels
By adding different metals to steel, new steels with different properties can be made. The following metals are added to steel to alter its properties.

ALUMINUM: Used to produce heat resistant steels.

CHROMIUM: Gives stainless properties and increases hardness and resistance to corrosion.

MANGANESE: Gives hardness and increased tensile strength to steel. It is used to de-oxidize steel so it is present in nearly all steels.

MOLYBDENUM: Adds strength, toughness and hardness, but does not affect the machinability of steel. Used to make high speed steel.

NICKEL: Increases strength and toughness and raises the impact resistance of steel.

SILICON: Increases resiliance and is used for making springs. It is also used to make steels resistant to heat, acid and electricity.

TUNGSTEN: Used to produce high speed steels to make cutting tools. Tungsten steel is "red hard," that is, it remains hard enough to cut even when it is red hot.

VANADIUM: Used in small quantities to increase hardness. With chromium it makes chrome-vanadium steel which is very strong and shock resistant and is used to make transmission parts and gear boxes.

NON-FERROUS METALS

Copper
Copper is a soft, reddish metal which is easy to cut and work and is the most suitable of all the decorative metals for beginners to work on. It can be beaten, soft and hard soldered, welded and forged and it takes a high polish. Copper conducts heat and electricity very well and therefore about half the world copper supply is used by the electricity industry, one quarter goes into the production of the many copper alloys which are some of the most useful metals we have. When it is exposed to damp air for long periods, copper becomes coated with green copper acetate. This verdigris as it is called, is very poisonous and any eating or drinking vessel made from copper must be given a protective coating of some kind, usually this consists of a thin coat of some non-toxic metal such as tin (see tinning page 125).

COPPER ALLOYS

Brass
Brass is an alloy of copper and about one third zinc. It is a soft, ductile, malleable, yellow metal which casts well. It is slightly more difficult to work than copper, although it can be worked hot or cold, soldered and brazed. It takes a very high polish. Brass is sometimes identified by the percentage of copper in the alloy, for example, brass 66 is an alloy of 66% copper, 34% zinc.

Bronze

Bronze was originally an alloy of copper and tin, but today tin is so expensive that plain bronze made only of copper and tin is quite rare, zinc or other metals are used instead. It is easy to cast and used to be used extensively for marine fittings, bells and bearings as well as for decorative work.

PHOSPHOR BRONZE: Contains a very small quantity of phosphor, about 0.5%, which makes the metal strong, tough and resistant to corrosion. It can be cast and drawn into wire and is used for bearings and springs.

ALUMINUM BRONZE: The addition of aluminum gives the metal about three times the strength of copper. It resists wear and corrosion at high temperatures and can be drawn, spun, forged, soldered and brazed. Because it is so resistant to corrosion it is used for fittings underwater and in sewage works.

Gilding metal

An alloy composed mainly of copper containing between 5% and 20% zinc. It is used mainly for beaten metalwork and inexpensive jewelry.

Nickel silver

Also known as German silver. Nickel silver is an alloy of copper and zinc which contains no silver and very little nickel. It is yellow-white in color and most commonly used as a base for silver plate. It is fairly easy to work but needs annealing and then cooling slowly if it is to be hammered.

Alpaca

A type of nickel silver, almost silver-white in color. It is quite commonly used in craft work.

Gunmetal

An alloy of copper, tin and zinc, it is reddish-yellow in color and polishes well, but darkens when exposed to the air. It is strong and tough, the strongest of the copper alloys. It resists corrosion and casts well. It is used as castings, steam-pipe fittings and marine fittings.

Aluminum

Until about 75 years ago, aluminum was very rare and expensive because of the difficult extraction process. Today, however, it is the most important metal after iron and steel. It is its light weight which makes aluminum such a useful metal, but pure aluminum is not very strong, so it is alloyed with other metals.

Aluminum is malleable, soft, ductile and an excellent conductor of electricity. It can be rolled out into very thin foil, spun, and drawn into wire, shaped and bent. Aluminum sheet is very easy for an amateur to work in a variety of ways. Aluminum cannot be soldered by the ordinary methods but it can be welded and brazed. It casts well and can be polished to a high finish.

Duralumin

An alloy containing several metals including copper, manganese and magnesium with about 94% aluminum. It is almost as strong as mild steel, with all the lightness of aluminum. However, it age hardens and corrodes. It bends, folds and is easy to work cold although it quickly work hardens and cannot be soldered by the usual methods. It can be forged, spun, stamped and hammered. It is used widely in the aerospace industries and for vehicle parts, and many components where lightness and strength are important.

Lead

A very heavy and very soft metal, bluish-gray in color. It can easily be rolled, bent, folded and cast. It can be joined by soft soldering and has a very low melting point. It resists corrosion well and is not affected by water or acids. It was often used for roofing, although today it is too expensive for this. It is used as sheathing and lining for cables and containers, for battery elements and piping. It is also used as a base for many alloys and as a component in soft solder. A small amount of lead is added to some steels and brasses to make them free cutting.

Lead is a very poisonous metal which can seriously affect people who use it carelessly. If you do any work with lead, avoid getting it in an open cut and avoid inhaling dust and fumes from it. Make sure the working area is well ventilated.

Nickel

Silvery-white in color, a strong metal which is very resistant to corrosion. In its pure state it is used for plating to form a protective layer under chromium. It is also an important alloy metal, and is added to steel to give strength to components, like gears, under stress.

Pewter

Originally pewter was an alloy of tin and lead, but because lead is poisonous, there is none in modern pewter. It is usually now made up of 95% tin with antimony and copper. Pewter is a soft and malleable metal that was once widely used for kitchen utensils. It is an ideal metal for decorative work as it is easy to work and casts well, but it has a low melting point and needs a special solder.

Tin

A bright, silvery metal, malleable but not strong, although it is very resistant to corrosion. It is now very expensive and is rarely used in its pure state. It is widely used for plating and is an important part of many alloys, including soft solder and bronze.

White metal

Also known as Babbitt metal and Antifriction metal, white metal is an alloy of tin, antimony and copper. It is quite a soft metal although harder than tin. It works well cold and casts well. Used mainly for bearings and for decorative work.

Zinc

Zinc is a blue-gray metal, almost as dense as steel. It is quite a hard and brittle metal, although it is easily bent and folded to shape. It has a low melting point of only 756°F (419°C). It becomes ductile at 212°F (100°C) to 300°F (150°C) and is therefore very easy to work when it is slightly warm, although at 393°F (200°C) it becomes brittle again. It can be soldered easily, but because of its low melting point, needs care. About half the world's zinc is used to make galvanized iron, the other important uses are as sheets for roofing and containers. It is a constituent of many alloys.

Gold

Gold is a soft, yellow, bright metal. It is the toughest, but at the same time the most easily forged of all metals. It is a very expensive jewelers' metal and it will not be used for any of the projects in this book.

Silver

Pure silver is soft, white, ductile, malleable and easy to work. The pure metal is too soft for most purposes and so is alloyed with copper to give it extra hardness. It can be beaten, wrought, cast and worked in many different ways. Sterling silver must contain 925 parts of pure silver to 1000 parts of alloy. Silver must be annealed if it is to be forged. It can be soldered, but only with hard or silver solder which contains 50% silver.

BUYING METAL

You can use a wide variety of metals for the techniques and projects in this book. Generally, you will be using the softer and more malleable metals—mild steel, wrought iron, aluminum, brass, copper, white metal, gilding metal and perhaps tin, pewter and silver. For a complete beginner to metalwork buying the metal may present quite a few problems. After all, materials for woodworking—tools, nails, screws and wood are all commonly on sale on ordinary do-it-yourself counters which are found everywhere. Some of these stores may possibly stock materials like sheet aluminum for household repairs. Craft stores too, are plentiful and these often sell art metals like copper and pewter. But where do you go to buy wrought iron, mild steel and brass! The problem for the craftworker needing only small quantities of these metals is that most firms supplying this kind of metal, supply only to the industry. Not only are they accustomed to selling large quantities, but they are not often easy to find.

The best way to begin looking for the right kind of supplier is to start with the Yellow Pages of the telephone book. If you live in a city or near a big industrial area you will have many more suppliers to choose from. Here are some likely categories which you could check in your telephone directory: alloy steel suppliers, aluminum suppliers, brass and copper suppliers, copper and copper alloys, iron and steel suppliers, pipes, sheet metal suppliers, steel makers, tubes and tube fitting and wrought ironwork.

Jewelers' and plumbers' suppliers are useful for many tools and materials. If you have difficulty finding specialist tools, these suppliers can often tell you where to buy them.

If you live in the country or anywhere with a large horse population, there will be a blacksmith somewhere in the area. You could ask him either to recommend a supplier of metal, or even ask if he will sell you a small amount of the metal he buys in large quantities.

Having tracked down a likely supplier, you now have to go about buying the metal from him. This may not always be very easy, especially when dealing with a firm used to selling large quantities of metal. What you will find is a large yard or warehouse with extensive stocks of materials. Most of the customers will be builders or other industries in the area who buy in large and regular quantities—larger certainly than the individual who only wants enough metal to make, say, a patio lamp.

Another thing that you will find is that customers to yards such as this are not at liberty to wander around looking at the stock. Customers are served by a warehouseman who comes to the counter, takes the order, and then disappears into the warehouse or yard to make up the order. This is then brought to the counter or sent to the dispatch bay. You will not be very welcome if you go along, expecting to be able to look at all the metals and then buy only a small piece. However, if the yard is not busy, someone will probably take you around the yard and let you look at the stock. But for your own safety, you will not be allowed to wander around at will. So it will save time and tempers all around if you find out as much as you can about the materials supplied by the company and the materials that you want before you go to buy.

A phone call to the company office often yields dividends—especially if the company has a catalog. If you can get hold of a catalog, you may be amazed to discover what a wide range of items the company sells—items that you might never even have considered asking about. Metal suppliers sometimes sell fittings that you cannot find in ordinary do-it-yourself stores, for example, wheels, links and heavy chains, or provide services such as cutting, sawing or applying protective coatings. They may also sell specialist tools. Another advantage of a catalog is it will give you some idea of the huge range of shapes and sizes in which bars, rods, tubes and extrusions are made in various metals.

You may of course, find a small or very friendly supplier who will be only too happy to tell you all you want to know, or you may live near a large do-it-yourself or craft supermarket which has all you need on display so that you can pick and choose at leisure. However, if your only choice is a large trade supplier, you will get most benefit from his wide range of stock if you find out as much as you can about what he supplies and what you want before you go.

A big metal warehouse sells large quantities of metal in many different shapes and sizes, but is usually willing to sell smaller quantities to individual customers

17

MEASURING SYSTEMS

The systems used for measuring metals, with their various gauges, can be confusing. The metric system, where measurements are in millimeters or in centimeters instead of inches and fractions of an inch, can make things even trickier. The United States, unlike Europe, is not fully metric although many of its measurements are. Some comparative tables between these systems are shown on pages 154–155. The terminology used for ordering metals too, can be a confusing foreign language for the amateur. Here are a few points which may clarify the situation.

The most important dimension of sheet metal is its thickness which can be anything from several inches to foil measured in thousandths of an inch. Below a certain point, fractions and thousandths of an inch become impossible and for the thinnest measurements a system of gauges is used. In England the Standard Wire Gauge (SWG) may be used for wire and sheet metal of all kinds. In the United States the Brown and Sharpe (B&S) or American Standard gauge is used for non-ferrous wire and sheet metals; while the United States Standard gauge (USS) is used for iron and steel. With all these gauges, the lower numbers denote thicker materials, the higher numbers thinner materials.

A gauge itself is a thin disk or rectangle of metal with slots cut in its edge. One side of the gauge shows the thickness as a whole number, the other side shows it in thousandths of an inch. The gauge of sheet metal or wire is indicated by the number of the slot (not the hole) into which the metal fits easily.

Metal may also be measured by the weight per square foot, or weight per square meter. In America, copper sheet for example, is sold by the weight per square foot. For example, 24 ounce copper, which weighs about $1\frac{1}{2}$ pounds per square foot is equal to 20 on the B&S gauge. Tin plate is measured by the USS gauge or by symbols, ICL, IC, IX, IXX to IXXXXXX. The more X's the thicker the plate.

Metal sheet materials are sold either in standard size sheets measured in feet or millimeters, or sometimes in rolls by the linear foot or meter. If the metal comes in standard size sheets, you may occasionally have to buy the whole sheet, but usually stockists are happy to sell small pieces or fractions of a sheet. With linear measures, one foot or one meter may be the smallest quantity you can buy.

When you order metal, always state clearly which gauge you are using. Also make sure that you know which gauge your supplier is refering to in his catalog or in the warehouse.

Sheet metals may also be sold as stamped blanks, that is, individual pieces cut out into a variety of standard shapes. Craft stores sell copper blanks, for enameling or

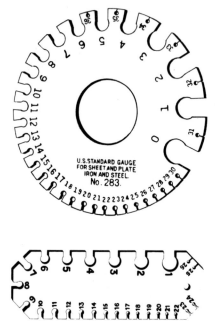

Top: a United States Standard gauge, used for measuring the thickness of iron and steel sheet
Above: a Standard Wire gauge, used in Britain for measuring wire and sheet metal of all kinds

other craftwork, already cut out into suitable shapes for pendants, earrings, brooches and rings. Trade suppliers sell a much larger range of blanks in other metals and in larger sizes. Blanks of this kind come in many different thicknesses, some more than an inch thick.

Tubes, pipes, sections and rods come in an almost infinite variety of shapes and sizes. If you can use a ready-made section, you will often save yourself a great deal of hard work, so it is worth trying to find out what shapes are available.

Most long sections are sold either in standard lengths or by the linear foot or meter. Again you will probably be able to buy small pieces and fractions of standard lengths, but you may not be able to buy fractions of linear measures.

Sections, like sheet are also usually measured by the pound per foot or kilogram per meter. Round stock is described by its diameter, as is hexagonal and octagonal stock. Bars are described by their width and depth; angles, U-sections and T-sections have three measurements, depth or height, width and thickness. Tubes and pipes are measured by their outside diameter (o.d.), read in inches or millimeters. The wall thickness is also measured by gauge.

When you are ordering sections, tubes, rods, and also wire, don't forget to state the gauge and include a clear description of the shape, whatever it is—round, hexagonal, T-shaped or angled.

Conversion tables

Some comparative tables between the inch and metric systems and the various gauge systems are given on pages 154–155. Below, are some conversion tables showing how you can convert from one system to another. With the help of a calculator, you can do this in seconds.

INCHES AND MILLIMETERS
To convert inches to millimeters multiply by 25.39977.
To convert millimeters to inches multiply by 0.03937.

OUNCES AND GRAMS
To convert ounces to grams multiply by 28.3495.
To convert grams to ounces multiply by 0.03527.

GALLONS AND LITERS
To convert gallons to liters multiply by 4.54102.
To convert liters to gallons multiply by 0.220215.

FAHRENHEIT AND CENTIGRADE
To convert Fahrenheit to centigrade, from the number of degrees F, subtract 32. Multiply the result by 5 and divide by 9.
To convert centigrade to Fahrenheit, multiply the degrees C by 9, divide by 5 and add 32.

CHAPTER TWO
The Workshop

If you intend making more than a single project in metal you need a space of your own in which to work. Metalwork is not something that can easily be done on a corner of the kitchen table—it is noisy, quite strenuous and requires potentially dangerous tools which are best not used where children and pets can interfere with your work. In any case, nothing is more tedious and time consuming than having to set up your tools and equipment and then clear everything away at each session.

Most metalwork projects you are likely to tackle are not large and metalwork can be done in quite a small space, providing the space is well organized. A well planned workspace pays off in years of pleasure, so before you begin, spend some time considering just where you will work. If you already have a space set aside for do-it-yourself or home repairs, this can easily be adapted.

No two home workshops are the same; each must be adapted to the space, time and money available, but there are a number of general factors to consider. First, how much time do you plan to spend on metalwork? Even occasional projects require a worksurface and a vise. You will also need enough space to do things such as sawing, filing and hammering, together with enough room to store your tools, a supply of metal and a few odd tools and pieces of equipment. Try and plan as much workshop space as possible. You will need a

good light source, both daylight and artificial light and at least two accessible electric outlets.

All of these requirements can be met by a walk-in closet or a space under the stairs and in an apartment this may be the best that you can do. Other places where you can set up a workshop could be in the attic, basement, garage or an outdoor shed. However, if you have no alternative but to use the kitchen table, or any table that is used for something else besides metalwork, get a protective covering that you can remove when the metalwork session is finished. Use an aluminum sheet or a sheet of $\frac{3}{8}$ to $\frac{1}{2}$ in. (9.5 to 12 mm.) plywood, and secure it to the table top with clamps. Have a piece of asbestos sheet too for extra protection during soldering and heating operations. Use soft asbestos, not hard building sheet, it may shatter when heated.

Wherever you decide to set up the workshop, take the following features into account.

THE FLOOR: You will be standing for most of the time so the floor must be well insulated, for safety as well as for warmth and comfort. If the workroom floor is concrete, the ideal covering is a wooden floor which you can make yourself of tongue and groove planking. Cover the concrete with tar paper and then nail planed 1 in. (25 mm.) pine boards to sleepers set 20 to 24 in. (505 to 600 mm.) apart. Adjust the sleepers with wedges so the flooring will be level. This type of floor

can be set up so that it provides a walkway only the length of the workbench if you wish. Cork, vinyl and carpet are also suitable.

ELECTRICITY FOR LIGHT AND HEAT
Try and arrange for the best lighting possible, both natural and artificial. If possible, position the workbench under a window and fix artificial lights over the window so you have a constant source of light. There should be a good source of light over the vise and a strong light for close, detail work. Spotlights on wall or ceiling tracks provide a good and flexible light source.

Make sure you have some means of heating the workshop in cold weather. Cover the walls with insulation board if they are bare wood or concrete. You should have at least two wall outlets for plugs. Check carefully when you buy power tools that they can be run safely off the household wiring system. You may need a separate circuit that can handle heavier loads. If the wiring system has to be set up specially for the new workshop—run up to the attic or out to a shed for example—it is wise to invest in the services of a professional electrician.

VENTILATION: Good ventilation is essential. Some processes, those using gas torches and acids for cleaning and coloring metal, give off fumes. Work with lead, which is poisonous, should always be done in a well ventilated area. You may

The ideal workshop, well-equipped,
with plenty of light and space.
Notice the heavy bench on the left
which supports a home-made anvil
cut from a length of railway track
(see page 54). Plenty of tool
racks, drawers and cupboards
mean that everything has a place,
leaving the worksurfaces clean and
uncluttered

want to fit an extractor fan as an extra precaution.

NOISE: A small point, but metalwork is often noisy, and you will not be popular if you disturb the rest of the family. Some insulation in your workroom could prevent any problems.

ACCESS: You should be able to get materials into the workshop and the finished project out again without any trouble. Metal rods and bars can be quite long and sheet materials awkward to maneuver. This should not be much of a problem unless you are working in a closet or an attic, where access may be by step ladder. Inaccessibility too is a point you should consider from the beginning. Thieves, children and pets must be kept out of the workshop. You will need either a locking tool chest or secure locks on the workshop doors and windows. A design for a simple tool cabinet which you can make yourself, and to which you can easily add a padlock, is shown on page 28.

STORAGE SPACE: Be as generous as you can at the planning stage. As you become more experienced and more interested in metalwork, you will gradually accumulate many more tools than you had to begin with, as well as building up a stock of metal. Plan to have more shelves and drawers than you think you will need. Metal rods, bars and extrusions can be stored on shelf

brackets which are angled slightly upwards to keep the stock against the wall. Sheet materials can be stored neatly against a wall and kept in place by a wooden batten fixed to the floor a few inches away from the wall.

Keep small items like screws, nails and washers in labeled cans or in glass jars. One or two large bins for storing odd shaped pieces of metal would also be useful. One last item, a stool is a good idea for the occasions when you want to sit at the workbench.

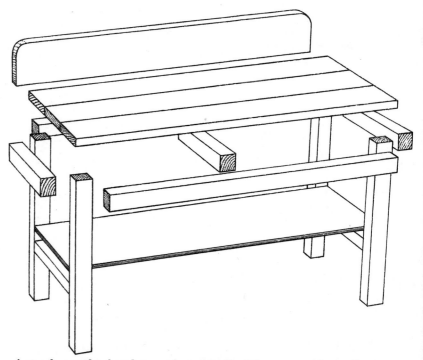

A sturdy wooden bench to make yourself. Ask your wood supplier to cut the pieces to length and the construction itself will be quick and simple

The workbench

The workbench is the single most important item in your workshop and the center of all activity. It must be strong and sturdy. Metalwork involves a lot of hammering, wrenching, twisting and bending. The metalwork bench has to provide a stable base for all these strenuous activities. The bench should be absolutely rigid, and should not vibrate during operations like drilling and filing. If the bench is made of wood, as most are, keep a sheet of aluminum or plywood to cover the top during operations involving heat. Your workbench will have a long life if you protect the top from cuts and burns. Some craftsmen screw a $\frac{1}{4}$ in. (6 mm.) thick sheet of plywood to the top of a new bench. As the extra top becomes worn it can be turned over, then eventually replaced.

The height of the bench is very important. Much work will be done at the vise and so you should adjust the height of the bench to take this into account. An average bench will stand around 3 feet (920 mm.) high, plus an extra 4 inches (100 mm.) for the vise.

There are many different kinds of benches available. Most do-it-yourself manuals give illustrations and plans for benches to build yourself, or you can buy a number of different kinds of bench. However, here are two basic types of workbench that you can build yourself, and one that you can buy in most do-it-yourself stores.

Wooden bench

All the pieces of the bench are softwood.

Legs: Four pieces 3 × 3 in. (75 × 75 mm.), 31 in. (793 mm.) long, adjust for your height.

Two cross pieces 2 × 4 in. (50 × 100 mm.), 24 in. (610 mm.) long.

Top: 3 planks, 2 × 10 in. (5 × 250 mm.), 60 in. (1525 mm.) long.

Two cross pieces, running from side to side, 2 × 4 in. (50 × 100 mm.), 50 in. (1270 mm.) long.

Three crosspieces running back to front 2 × 4 in. (50 × 100 mm.). 24 in. (610 mm.) long.

Back plate: 1 × 6 × 60 in. (25 × 150 × 1525 mm.).

Shelf: 1 in. (25 mm.) thick plywood, 24 × 60 in. (610 × 1525 mm.).

Assemble the two pairs of legs with their cross pieces. Assemble the bench top and its cross pieces. Attach the top pieces to the frame with heavy countersunk screws. Screw the back plate to the top. Screw the shelf to the cross pieces. The shelf not only provides a useful storage space, it gives the bench added stability and rigidity.

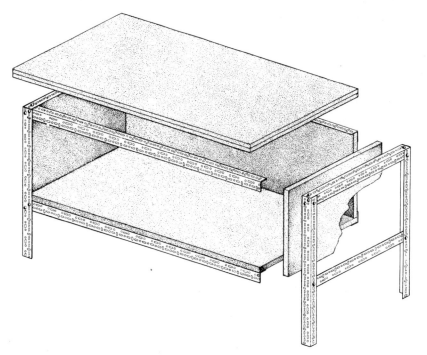

A bench made of metal angles bolted together is strong and practical. The worksurface consists of thick chipboard sheet

Metal bench

A bolt-together metal frame, covered with blockboard or chipboard is quick to make and very sturdy. If you buy the metal angles cut to length, you can put this bench together in an afternoon.

Legs: Four pieces, 31 in. (793 mm.) long, adjust for your height. Cross pieces: Four for the sides, 24 in. (610 mm.) long, four for front and back, 54 in. (1370 mm.) long. Top: Two pieces $\frac{3}{4}$ in. (18 mm.) thick chipboard, 28 × 56 in. (710 × 1422 mm.), screw them together to make a thick, strong top.

Two side pieces, 1 in. (25 mm.) thick chipboard, 20 × 24 in. (505 × 610 mm.). Back: 1 in. (25 mm.) thick chipboard, 20 × 54 in. (505 × 1370 mm.).
Shelf: $\frac{3}{4}$ in. (18 mm.) thick chipboard, 24 × 54 in. (610 × 1370 mm.).

Bolt together the side frames and cross pieces. Bolt the upper side pieces to the legs, flush with the top. Bolt the front and back pieces to the side frames, fitting the two back rails first. Bolt the lower shelf in place and then fix the side and back panels. Position the top to overlap the front sufficient to fit the vise.

The Workmate, a folding metal bench with a wooden top consisting of two vise-like jaws is strong, inexpensive and versatile. When not in use it can be folded up and hung on the wall

Workmate

This ready-made bench is ideal if space is limited. It is strong, inexpensive and available everywhere. The bench top is a giant vise and the jaws, which are 27 in. (685 mm.) long, open 3 in. (75 mm.) wide. The bench is well balanced, does not wobble and by standing on the base you can give it the extra stability required for metalwork. The Workmate folds flat and so is ideal if you have limited space.

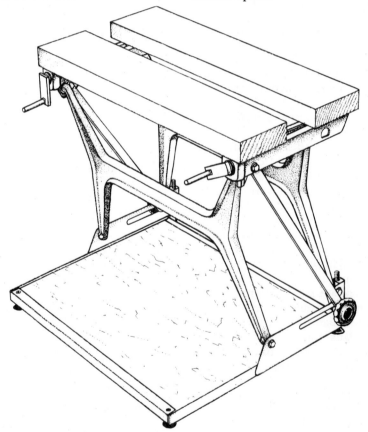

Buying tools

There are two important points to remember when you buy tools. Buy each tool only as and when you need it and buy the best tool you can afford. Good tools are in themselves beautiful, sturdy and functional and you will get great pleasure and a lifetime's service from a collection of used and useful tools built up over the years.

Always buy tools made by a reputable manufacturer. Be wary of tools that carry no brand name, especially if you do not have the experience to judge a tool by its weight and feel. Good tools are always made from quality steel and the working surface has been hardened and ground to the correct degree.

Buy the right kind of tools for metalwork. If you have a collection of tools that you have been using for woodwork or general repairs around the house, not all of them will be tough enough to stand up to metalworking. For instance, a metalworking chisel is very different from a carpenter's chisel. You should in any case never use a tool except for the job for which it is intended. Never be tempted to improvise—using a screwdriver handle as a hammer or a drill as a center punch, for example. This is not only dangerous, but will ruin a good tool.

Finally, don't be afraid to ask for advice when buying tools. The staff in a good hardware store know their stock and will be pleased to tell you about it.

Caring for tools

The use and care of individual tools is covered in detail in a later chapter, but here are some general points on caring for your tool collection.

Check tools regularly to make sure that cutting edges are sharp and that handles fit properly and are not loose or cracked. Check for rust spots, and if any appear rub them away with emery cloth or steel wool and then re-condition the metal by rubbing well with oil. Rust can spoil a good tool in a very short time, so don't forget to make regular checks, especially of those tools that you only use occasionally.

Get into the habit of rubbing each tool over with an oily rag, kept specially for the purpose, after you have finished using it.

Keep a lump of chalk in a tool box or drawer to absorb excess moisture. Be extra careful if the workshop is damp or humid.

Protect the cutting edges of sharp tools. Chisels are often sold with their own plastic blade guards. You can improvise blade guards for saws and chisels from plastic garden hose. Cut a piece of hose the length of the blade, then slit it down one side and fit it over the cutting edge.

Storing tools

Each tool that you own should have a place where it is kept when not in use. Tools should never be thrown together in a drawer or tool bag or box. Most tools can be hung up and if possible they should be. There are all kinds of simple tool boards and racks which you can devise and set up yourself, as well as a number which you can buy.

Hammers, wrenches, snips, shears, squares and many other tools can be hung up using a little ingenuity. Saws should be hung downwards, suspended by their handles on blocks of wood or dowel pegs. Soldering irons, which may still be hot, should be hung from metal hooks. Drills are usually sold in sets in their own plastic or metal case. If you do not buy a set, you can make a drill stand from a block of wood or metal into which you should drill a hole to take each drill.

Tools which must be stored flat, like files, should each be wrapped in a cloth and stored in a drawer where they will not be able to slide around and knock into each other. You could use an old cutlery basket to store tools of this type.

Tool storage boards

The simplest tool storage board of all can be made simply from a sheet of $\frac{1}{2}$ in. (12 mm.) thick chipboard, cut to fit the available space and fixed to the wall. Hang tools as shown, either between two nails, or on dowel pegs or hooks. For instant identification, outline each tool with paint, in this way you will know instantly if a tool is missing from its place. You can also use pegboard, which comes already perforated and with special hooks for hanging tools, instead of chipboard.

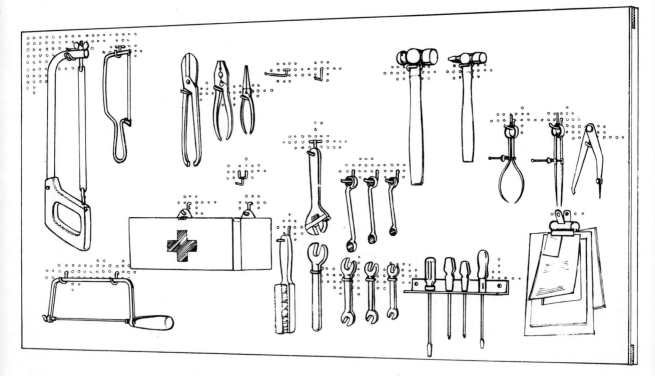

Pegboard provides an inexpensive and flexible means of hanging tools

26

Tool racks

Fixing up tool racks around the workshop to suit your own collection of tools is a job where you can enjoy exercising your ingenuity. You can make a very simple tool rack for bladed tools, like screwdrivers, from a length of angle iron. On one face of the iron drill holes and cut slots as required to fit the tools. Drill screw holes on the other face and fix the rack to the wall. A rack like this makes an ideal simple first project and will help you to get the feel of metal as you cut and drill it to suit your own requirements. A tool rack like this, ready drilled with a variety of holes and slots of different sizes is available in many hardware stores if you prefer to buy a rack.

Another type of rack can be made from two wooden battens kept parallel to each other by spacers. The tools slot down between the battens. Nail and glue spacers between the battens at regular intervals. To finish, screw a sheet of plywood or clear plastic over the outer batten as a blade guard.

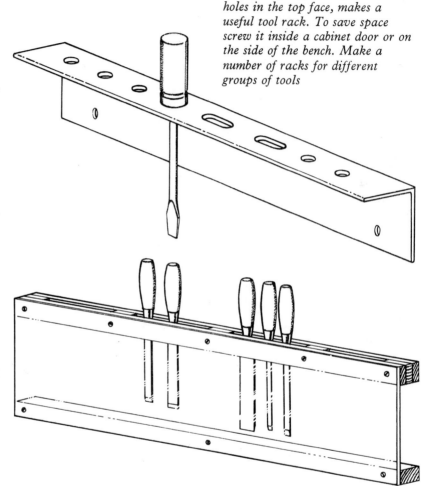

A length of angle iron, with drilled holes in the top face, makes a useful tool rack. To save space screw it inside a cabinet door or on the side of the bench. Make a number of racks for different groups of tools

A rack with a clear plastic blade guard is a good way of storing sharp bladed tools. The cutting edges are well protected and you can see at a glance that everything is in its place. You can make a similar rack for other tools, omitting the lower batten and cover

27

Tool closet

If space is restricted, or if you are unable to make the whole workshop secure against thieves and children, then a locking tool closet is a good idea. You can make one yourself like the closet shown. Use $\frac{1}{2}$ in. (12 mm.) thick plywood for the frame and shelves, and $\frac{1}{4}$ in. (6 mm.) thick plywood for the back and the two doors.

You can easily adapt this design to fit the space available in the workshop and to house your own collection of tools. Begin by making an accurate scale drawing of the basic frame. Plan out the arrangement of shelves, pegs, racks and drawers.

Begin by making the box shape for the back, gluing and nailing the sides together, then nail on the back.

The rack at the top is made by drilling holes through a $\frac{1}{2}$ in. (12 mm.) thick piece of plywood. Glue and nail the plywood to the back of the cabinet and insert lengths of dowel through the holes, securing them with glue.

The shelf supports are made from $\frac{1}{4}$ in. (6 mm.) thick pieces of wood glued to the sides of the box, with spaces between them allowing the shelves to slide in. Small drawers are simple-to-construct boxes with a hole in the front.

Make the doors in the same way and fit them to the back with lengths of continuous hinge. Fix a padlock across the doors to make the cabinet secure. Hang the cabinet on the wall with two mirror brackets fixed to the top. If it is particularly large or heavy, give it extra support by fixing a batten to the wall beneath. Finish the cabinet with a coat of clear varnish.

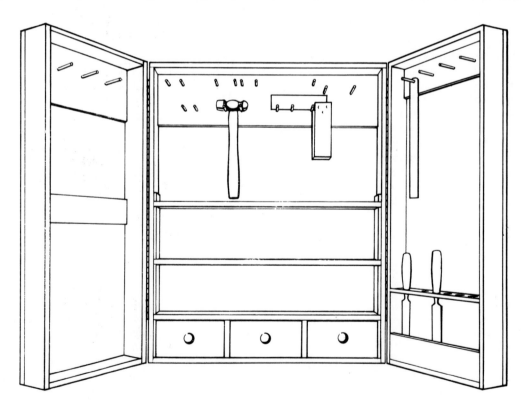

Safety in the workshop

Practice safe working procedure from the very beginning so that it becomes a habit.

Begin safety checks with yourself. Always dress so that there are no loose cuffs or ties to flap around, no pieces of jewelry, rings or watches to get caught in moving tools. Be sure long hair is tied back so it's not in your eyes.

Keep a pair of overalls, a coat or an apron in the workshop so that you can easily slip them on as you walk in. Always wear goggles when using a grinding wheel or in operations where sparks are formed or metal chips flying around. Wear rubber soled shoes when working with power tools.

Keep the workshop clean and neat and do not let pieces of metal lie around on the floor where you may slip on them, or on the bench, where they may cut your hands or damage a tool. Keep a bin handy beside the bench into which you can throw all small scraps and pieces of metal as you work. You can sort them out and put the ones you decide to keep into more permanent storage later. Even tiny pieces of metal can be useful for making washers, handles, feet, and so on.

Swarf, the metal shavings formed during drilling and cutting operations, can be sharp. Do not brush it away with your hand. Keep a small hand brush or a large, old paint brush by the bench for sweeping the work surface. Do this regularly as filings and grit can spoil and scratch your work.

Make sure your electric system conforms to safety regulations. Make sure that lights are bright enough to see exactly what you are doing at all times. Get a small fire extinguisher and a first aid kit and keep them in an obvious place, on the wall facing or beside the door for example, so that they can be seen immediately by anyone who comes in.

Before you start a project, get out all the tools you will need. Make sure that you have the right tools for the job so that you won't be tempted to improvise. Check that all cutting tools are sharp. If not, sharpen them before you begin work. You have to strain with a blunt tool and so have less control over the tool. Check that all handles are securely fixed and that there is no oil or grease on the handles. Put each tool away as you finish with it.

When using any cutting or pointed tools, make sure that the cutting edge is facing away from you, and that all force is exerted in the direction away from you. Use a vise or clamps to hold work, never your hands.

Never let pets into the workshop. Keep children out while you are working—in fact don't let children in at all unless you are prepared to teach them the correct way to use the tools they find. Have a secure locking system, either on the whole shop or on a large enough tool closet so that all your tools are safely locked away.

CHAPTER THREE

Basic tools and working techniques

MEASURING AND MARKING TOOLS

Steel rule

A steel rule is essential for measuring and marking out. Rules come in various sizes and with a wide choice of gradations. The most useful size is 12 in. (305 mm.) long with both inch and millimeter gradations. Rules are made either of carbon steel, or stainless steel which is worth buying, although it is slightly more expensive. Hang the rule up by the hole at one end so it is always on hand and in no danger of being scratched or bent if it is left lying around the workshop.

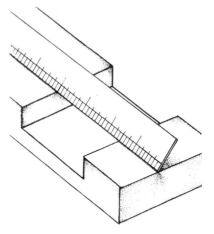

For really accurate measuring, hold the steel rule at an angle

Engineer's square

This tool is used for marking out and checking right angles and for checking the squareness of edges. The stock and blade form a true right angle. Made from carbon steel, the best types have hardened and ground faces. Sizes vary from 2 in. (50 mm.) up to 24 in. (610 mm.), the size is measured by the length of the blade. For accuracy when marking, place the point of the scriber (see page 32) in position and move the square up to the scriber rather than the other way around. Hang the try square up on two or three pegs when it is not in use (see drawing, page 28).

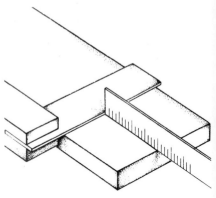

Above: Using the try square in combination with the rule to be sure measurements are taken from a square line

Left: Steel rule marked in millimeter gradations, try square and combination square. The protractor head and center square are on the rule, the square head lies beside them

Combination square

A set of four instruments in one, this is a very useful tool although it is not accurate enough for real precision work. It consists of a steel rule, grooved along the center or along one side. The three heads slide along the groove and can be locked in any position on it by means of knurled nuts.

The square head has one edge at 90 degrees and one at 45 degrees to the rule. It can be used as a square, a miter square, depth gauge and marking gauge. There is also a spirit level in the head; when the spirit level is horizontal, the work is vertical. The protractor head can be used to mark and check any angle up to 180 degrees. It contains a spirit level. The center square is used for finding the center of round stock.

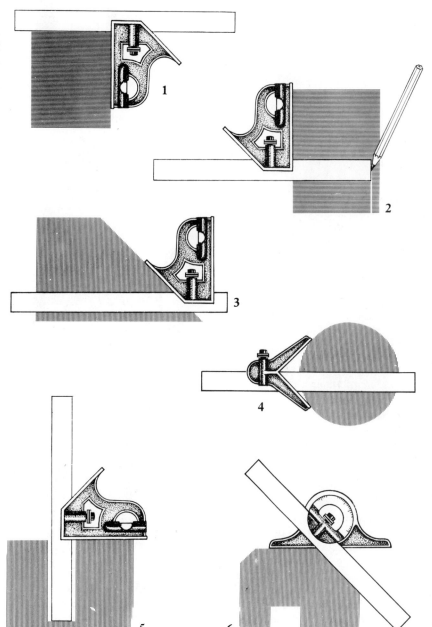

The versatile combination square has many uses, as shown here
1. Using the square head to check a right angle
2. Using the square head as a marking gauge
3. Checking a 45° angle with the square head
4. Finding the center of a bar using the center square
5. Measuring the depth of a recess using the square head
6. Using the protractor head to mark an angle

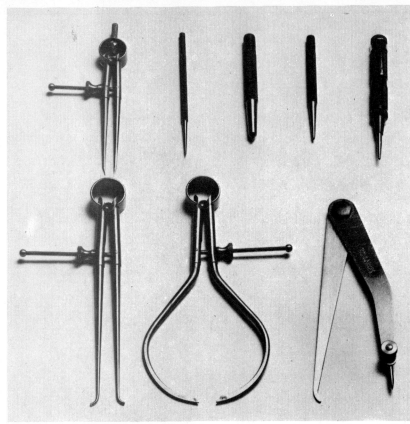

Dividers

Use dividers to describe circles and arcs, step off distances and to transfer measurements from a rule. The spring type which can be adjusted and held by a screw thread is the most useful. It is made from carbon steel with hardened and tempered points.

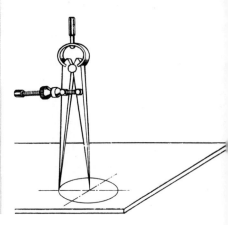

Top row (from left to right): Dividers, scriber, center punch, dot punch and automatic punch. Bottom row: Inside, outside and odd leg calipers

Using dividers to scribe a circle Notice that the center of the circle has been marked by scribed lines intersecting at right angles

Scriber

A scriber is used like a pencil to mark lines on metal. It is made in various shapes and sizes from high carbon steel with a hardened and tempered point.

Keep the point sharp so the scriber makes a fine and accurate line. You don't need to press hard, only use enough pressure to give you a visible line. Metal could crack along a deeply scribed line if it is bent. Don't use a scriber on surfaces that will show on the outside of the finished piece, use a pencil instead.

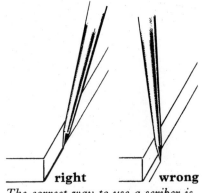

right   **wrong**

The correct way to use a scriber is to angle the point in against the rule

Punches

Punches are made from high quality tool steel hardened and tempered so that the point will withstand continuous use and the striking end will not splinter.

The center punch is used to mark the position for a drill before drilling begins. Hold the punch vertical and tap it with a hammer, making a light punch mark first. Deepen it only after the position has been checked for accuracy. Center punches are available with round or square heads.

An automatic center punch is spring loaded; it does not have to be hit with a hammer. Simply press down and the spring provides the power to punch the metal. The depth of the impression is variable and can be adjusted by turning a knob at the top. It does the same job as a standard center punch for about four times the price.

The dot or prick punch is similar to the center punch but it has a finer point. It is used to make small dents to locate lines, corners and circles. The points of all punches must be kept sharp.

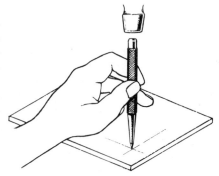

Making a center punch mark accurately at the intersection of two scribed lines

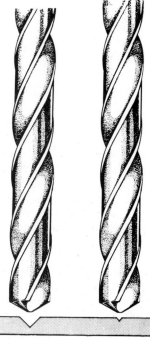

right   **wrong**

A center punch mark should be deep enough and wide enough to provide an accurate location for the edge of the drill. Left, the correct way; right, the punch mark is not deep enough

Calipers

For general work the odd leg, also known as jenny and hermaphrodite calipers are most useful. They are used to mark a line parallel to the edge of a piece of work or to find the center of the end of a bar. Inside calipers are used for checking inside diameters, outside calipers for checking outside diameters. You will not have much call for them unless you do precision work.

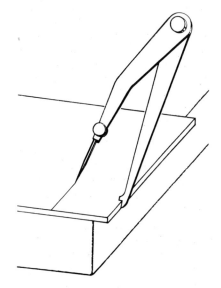

Using odd leg calipers to scribe a line a constant distance from an edge. With thin sheet, let the edge of the metal overhang the bench

HOLDING TOOLS
Vise

A bench vise is an essential piece of equipment in metalwork. Vises come in a variety of sizes, specified by the length and width of the jaws. You can buy vises with a swivel base and with a quick release mechanism, but these refinements are not essential and will not stand up to heavy work. The vise should be bolted to the workbench so that the front edge of the fixed rear jaw projects about ¾ in. (18 mm.) over the front edge of the bench. In this way you can clamp long objects into the jaws so that they do not touch the edge of the bench.

Buy the largest and heaviest bench vise that you can afford. You will be doing some work on the vise for almost every project and the vise will receive more wear than almost anything else in the workshop. A heavy vise is necessary if you plan to do a lot of beaten metalwork (see Chapter 8). Most stakes (the former over which the metal blank is hammered to shape) are supported in a vise, and a lightweight vise will vibrate under the heavy hammering required for this kind of work.

Vise jaws

The jaws give a parallel grip through their full movement. The jaw plates are made of hardened steel serrated on the inside to grip securely. They are fixed in place with countersunk screws and so can be removed and replaced. The jaws may mark softer metals so

they can be replaced with soft fiber or nylon jaws which you can buy or can be covered with vise clamps of soft metal which are very easy to make (see diagram). If you have no vise clamps you can always use wood or paper in the jaws to protect soft metals. You can also buy grooved jaws for holding pipes and round stock.

Using and caring for a vise

Always keep the vise clean and free of filings. Oil the screw occasionally. Never use the vise as an anvil for hammering and never tighten the jaws with a hammer or wrench as this will strain the screw.

A good, sturdy bench vise with 5¼ in. (135 mm.) jaws. It should be bolted to the edge of the bench so that the screw and handle hang clear

Vise clamps made by the vise manufacturer. The soft fiber pads are replaceable and are fixed to the clamps with countersunk screws

Leg vise

A leg vise is a heavy duty vise used by blacksmiths. The leg is fixed to the floor or to a fixture on the bench and so absorbs the shocks and rough use of forgework. When the vise is opened, the outer jaw swings in an arc so that parallel grip is only possible in one position, the leg vise will therefore not hold the workpiece as firmly as the bench vise with parallel grip. It is clumsy but strong. It may be difficult to find a leg vise to buy, although you should certainly try to acquire one if you plan to do forgework.

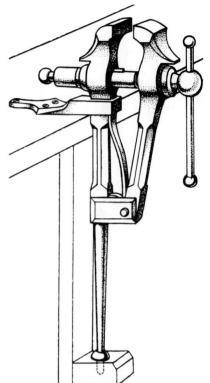

A leg vise fixed to a support on the bench. On some models the leg extends down to the floor

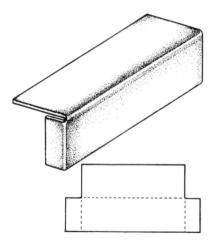

You can easily make simple vise clamps to this patten to fit over the jaws of your vise. Use a soft metal like copper or use cardboard

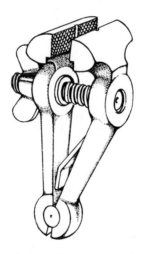

A hand vise, miniature version of the leg vise, can be useful occasionally

Hand vise

A hand vise works on the same principle as the leg vise. Useful for small pieces of work and for holding thin metal for drilling or riveting. Only buy one if you find you need it and cannot substitute a less expensive clamp (see page 36) for the job.

Pliers

Pliers are useful general purpose tools for holding, bending and making small adjustments. They are made in many shapes and sizes, for quite specialist purposes. Their size is denoted by their overall length; 6 in. to 8 in. (150 mm. to 200 mm.) are common sizes.

COMBINATION PLIERS: These are the most useful general pliers. They have a straight nose for gripping flat material, a round portion for holding round stock of small diameter, and cutting edges for cutting wire.

FLAT NOSE PLIERS: These pliers are used for holding flat materials.

ROUNDNOSE PLIERS: This tool is used for gripping and bending.

ENDCUTTERS: Strictly speaking these are not pliers, they are used for cutting wire.

Clamps

Every workshop needs some clamps as they are invaluable for performing all kinds of holding jobs. Gradually build up a collection of different sizes.

TOOLMAKERS CLAMPS: These are also called parallel clamps as they have a parallel grip throughout their movement. They are used for holding small pieces together during assembly operations like

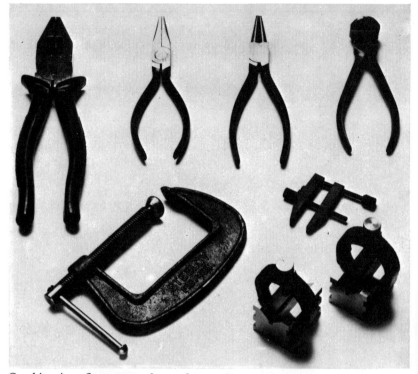

Combination, flat nose and round nose pliers, end cutters and clamps

screwing and riveting, or during drilling or marking out.

C-CLAMPS: These are used for clamping pieces together and for clamping metal to the bench for drilling and marking out.

V-BLOCK AND CLAMPS: V-blocks are made in pairs and are used for supporting round stock for marking out or drilling. Small sizes are provided with a pair of clamps for holding the work. Larger sizes don't need clamps as the weight of the metal is enough to hold it in position on the block.

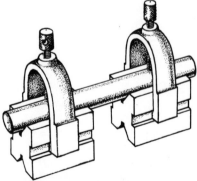

A pair of V-blocks supporting a round bar. The vertical screw in the clamps secures the bar in the V.

36

CUTTING TOOLS

Chisels

Chisels are made from lengths of octagonal-shaped high carbon steel or from harder alloy steels so they will withstand arduous work without fracturing. The head is left soft to withstand the shock of hammer blows, and is chamfered to slow down burring caused by hammering. Never use a chisel with a flattened "mushroom" head.

Chisel blades can easily be sharpened with a file (see page 58). File off burrs as soon as they occur.

HALF ROUND CHISEL: This chisel is used for cutting rounded grooves. It can also be used to correct a wandering drill (see page 46).

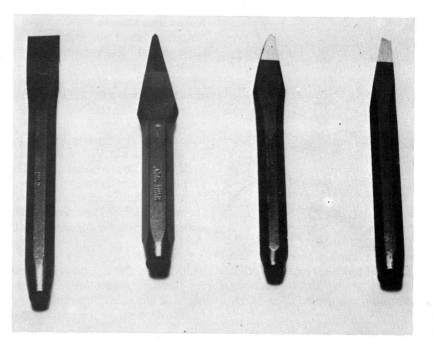

Left to right: Flat cold chisel, half round chisel, cross cut and diamond point chisels

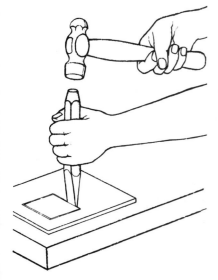

FLAT COLD CHISEL: This is used for cutting where saw or snips are not suitable, for cutting out holes and slots in sheet metal, for shearing metal in a vise, for shearing off rusted nuts and rivets.

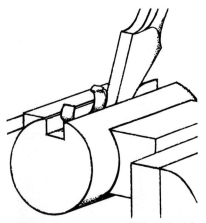

CROSS CUT CHISEL: This chisel is used for cutting grooves in solid metal. The chisel narrows behind the cutting edge for clearance when cutting the grooves.

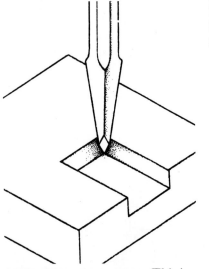

DIAMOND POINT CHISEL: This is a specialist chisel used for cleaning out corners, it too may be used for correcting a wandering drill.

Snips and shears

Snips are used for cutting thin sheet metal. They work with a scissor action. They should not be used for cutting wire. All cutting should be done with the back of the jaws never with the tips as they tend to leave a ragged edge. To cut with snips, open the jaws as wide as possible and put the metal as far back as you can. Make a cut as far as the middle of the jaws then open them wide and start again. When cutting to a scribed line, line up the cutting edge of the upper jaw with the line.

STRAIGHT SNIPS: These are used for cutting straight lines and large external curves. The length of the handle determines the leverage, so buy the largest you can afford, at least 12 in. (305 mm.) long. For greater leverage you can place the lower handle on the bench or hold it in the vise and press down.

CURVED SNIPS: These are also known as hawkbilled snips and are used for cutting internal curves only. Curved snips are used for more detailed work than straight snips and so do not have to be as large as straight snips.

UNIVERSAL SNIPS: As the name implies these are the most generally useful snips as they cut any shape except small inside curves.

GOSCUT: The goscut shears through sheet metal without distorting it. The fine toothed blade removes a thin strip of metal equal

To get more leverage when cutting sheet metal, secure one handle of the snips in the vise and press down

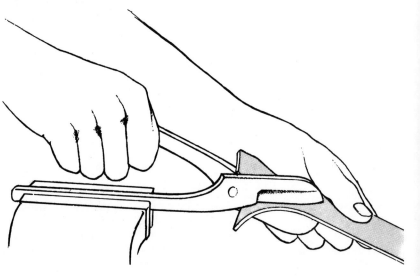

to its own width and therefore the blades do not get jammed in the middle of long cuts like snips do. With snips, you have to pull apart the metal on either side of the cut to make long cuts and this distorts it. Remember to take the width of the cut into account for precise measurements. The goscut has a second blade for cutting curves and circles, and another for cutting plastic laminate, hardboard and plywood.

Left to right: Curved snips, straight snips and the goscut fitted with the sheet metal cutting blade. Beside it is the blade for cutting laminates, plywood and hardboard and the blade used for cutting circles and curves.
Below: A pair of universal snips

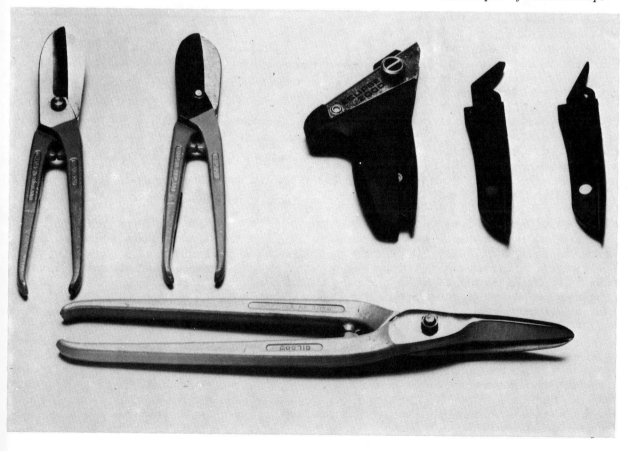

Hacksaw

A hacksaw is a general purpose cutting tool which can cut only in straight lines.

The frame can be fixed, or adjustable to fit blades 10 in. to 12 in. (250 mm. to 305 mm.) long. The handle can either be straight, like a file handle or have a pistol grip. Use whichever shape you find most comfortable to work with.

Blades

Blades are fixed into the frame by a wing nut. The type of blade you need for each job can vary widely according to the type and thickness of the metal to be cut.

Blades are classified by the number of teeth per inch (or 25 mm.) and by grade. The number of teeth per inch depends on the thickness and type of metal being cut. As a general rule the teeth should never straddle the material and at least three consecutive teeth must always be in contact with the metal.

Widely spaced teeth are unsuitable for cutting thin metal as they will straddle the thickness of the metal and probably snap. To saw thick metal, use the coarsest blade available to speed up the work. A coarse blade also clogs less easily when you are working with soft metal. A fine blade is best for harder metals like steel. The following is a general guide to the number of teeth per inch suitable for use with the various metals.

Teeth per inch

14: very soft metal like brass, copper and aluminum

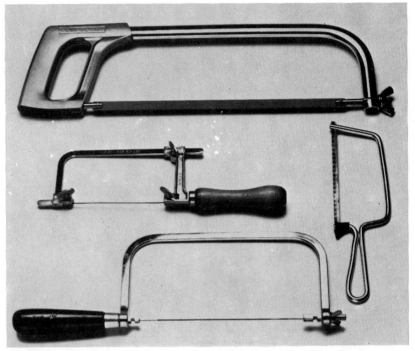

From top to bottom: Hacksaw with pistol grip handle; Piercing saw (left) and junior hacksaw (right) and abrafile

18: cast iron, mild steel and general work
24: hard metals
32: thin tubing, thin sheet steel

Grades of blades

The grade of a blade depends on the metal from which it is made. There are three types available. Flexible blades are made from low tungsten steel and only the teeth are hardened. This is the best blade for beginners to use as it is difficult to break.

All-hard blades are made of hardened and tempered tungsten steel which is brittle, but harder.

High speed steel blades are the most expensive grade. They are brittle but they last longest, unless the user is inexperienced, when they tend to snap easily. They can cut really hard metals.

Fitting blades

Fit a blade with the teeth facing forward, away from the handle so that it cuts on the forward stroke. Tension the blade by taking up the slack on the wing nut then make three full turns. You cannot sharpen hacksaw blades, but they are quite inexpensive to replace.

Using a hacksaw

Secure the work firmly in the vise. Stand at an angle of 45 degrees to the vise and hold the saw so that the frame is in line with your forearm. Steady the frame with your other hand. Make a few short backward strokes to establish the cut. Then saw with the whole length of the blade, cutting on the forward stroke and releasing pressure on the back stroke. Always try and cut with the blade kept horizontal.

Cut to the waste side of a scribed line and smooth off to the exact dimension with a file. Occasionally lubricate the blade lightly with oil or water to cool it off and to assist cutting.

To saw thin metal, clamp it between pieces of waste wood and saw through the sandwich. To cut brass, use a new blade as a worn one is likely to slip. To cut thick sections, saw from all sides, working in toward the center.

To cut a wide groove in thick metal, fit several blades side by side onto the saw and saw with them all together for the required depth of the groove. All the teeth should point forward.

Faults in sawing

If the cut wanders or the blade jams in the metal, you are probably twisting the blade out of line with the cut. Crooked cutting is the result of insufficient tension of the blade in the frame caused by either too much pressure on the strokes, or the work not being held firmly enough.

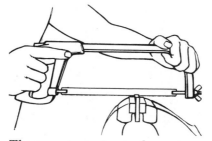

The correct way to use the hacksaw, with the frame in line with your forearm

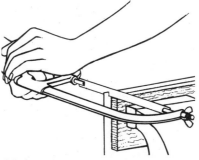

Make a long cut in sheet metal with the blade turned through 90°

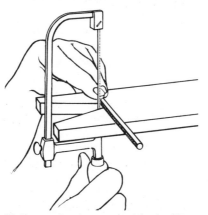

Using a piercing saw with the V-cut piercing table

Other types of saw

JUNIOR HACKSAW: This is used for lighter work, where a hacksaw would be too clumsy.

TENSION FILES: The commonest is an abrafile. It is made from tough, heat-treated steel wire. The blade is flexible and will cut in any direction. It is used for cutting intricate or irregular shapes. The blade fits onto a hacksaw frame with its own special clip-on links.

PIERCING SAW: A deep frame saw which holds a fine, flexible blade. Piercing is the process of cutting from the inside of the work, often in decorative patterns. This saw is used for intricate work, particularly on silver, copper, brass and aluminum.

Using a piercing saw

Start the cut by drilling a hole in the metal and then threading the blade through the hole and fitting it in the frame. The cutting action is up and down, with the teeth pointing downward. Most piercing work is hand held on a special wooden piercing table which has a wide V cut out of the front to allow the blade free movement and also to provide support for the metal on either side of the cut.

Clamp the piercing table in the vise and sit, so that the top of the piercing table is just below your shoulder. Keep the blade perpendicular at all times. Rubbing a candle on the blade will help to prevent it from sticking.

Files

Filing is used to finish and smooth metal and to give an accurate finish. Files are classified by length, section and cut. Length is measured from the shoulder above the file tang, the pointed metal at the end onto which a handle is fitted, to the tip. Most files are 4 in. to 18 in. (100 mm. to 460 mm.) long.

Section describes the shape of the section of steel from which the file is made. In some cases files are described by the use for which they are intended. The cut of a file varies from very coarse to extremely smooth.

Types of files

The flat file tapers towards the tip. It is a general purpose file.

The hand file is parallel throughout its length. It has one plain, uncut, or "safe" edge which allows you to work up to a corner without damaging the adjacent surface. It is used for flat surfaces.

The half round file has one flat and one curved face.

A square file is used for square holes and slots.

A round file tapers towards the tip. It is used for easing out holes and rounding slots. Small round files are called rat's tail files.

The three-square or triangular file is wedge-shaped in section. It is used for awkward corners and angles less than 90 degrees.

Needle files are small files made in many different shapes and usually sold in sets. They are used for fine work by jewelers, silver-

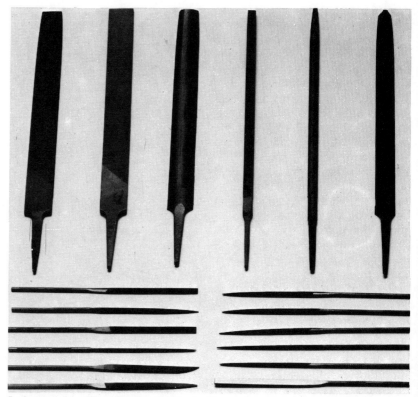

Left to right: Flat file, hand file, half round, square, round and three-square files. Below: A set of needle files

smiths and watchmakers.

Cut

File teeth are cut in a variety of patterns: single cut, double cut, rasp cut and curved tooth.

With single cut, the teeth are cut at an angle, running in diagonal rows across the file. These files are used for cutting hard metals.

In a double cut, a second set of teeth are made across the first. This cut is used for general work.

In rasp cut files each tooth is cut out separately. This type of cut is used for coarse work on soft metals.

A curved tooth file is a very coarse cut file used for soft metals.

Grade

The grade of a file indicates the coarseness of the teeth. The more teeth per inch (25 mm.) the smoother the cut. The grades available are rough and bastard cut for heavy removal of material, second cut for general purpose light removal, and smooth and

File cuts (from left to right): single cut, double cut, rasp cut, and coarsest of all, the curved tooth file

dead smooth for fine finishing work.

How to file

Good filing is skilled work as it is not easy to file a surface perfectly flat and smooth. The tendency is to rock the file which results in a rounded surface. Clamp the metal close to the area you will be filing, to cut down on vibration. Do not file in short strokes, use the whole length of the file in a slow, even motion maintaining constant pressure. At the end of the forward stroke lift the file and draw back. Cut only on the forward stroke or you will ruin the file. If you file continually in the same direction with a coarse file, you may produce a serrated surface on the metal which matches the teeth of the file. Shift the direction slightly on each

stroke.

Use the rough or the bastard file until nearly all the waste metal is removed. Then use the second cut file to remove the marks left by the rough file. Finish off to size with a smooth file by drawing it across the work in a process called drawfiling.

Drawfiling

Drawfiling is a finishing process used after cross filing. Hold a smooth or dead smooth file at right angles to the metal and push the file back and forth along the length of the workpiece. Keep your hands as close together as possible to reduce wobble.

Care and safety

"Pinning" is the metal worker's word for the clogging of file teeth with bits of metal. This can spoil the file and score the metal you are

working on. It is particularly likely to happen with soft metals. Clean the file with a wire brush or a file card which is a bed of needle points specially made for cleaning files. Rubbing chalk over the file helps to prevent pinning.

Never use a new file to remove the scale off castings or on welded or brazed joints or a burned soldering iron because you will ruin the teeth on this work. Use new files on brass and soft cast iron because the sharp teeth bite better.

File teeth are brittle and easily broken, so handle and store files carefully. Always fit a handle on a file. It is both safer and easier to use a file if it has a handle because the tang could easily pierce your hand. To fit a handle, slip the tang into the hole in the handle and tap the handle on the bench.

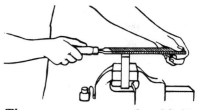

The correct way to stand and hold the file while cross filing

Hold the file close to the work on each side when drawfiling

Drilling

The twist drill, held either in a hand turned brace or in a power drill is the tool used for most metal drilling. Twist drills are best for thicker metal rather than thin sheet metal. The drill tends to go out of true on sheet metal, making a triangular rather than a round hole and forming burrs on the underside of the sheet metal. It is usually easier to punch a hole in sheet metal.

Types of twist drill

There are two grades of twist drill. Carbon steel is inexpensive, but it is likely to lose its temper when it becomes overheated. High speed steel drills are more expensive but they are red hard, and can be used in a power drill at high speed. You will need them to drill steel.

Two grooves, or flutes run around the body of the twist drill. They leave room for swarf to escape upward and for lubricating and cooling fluid to flow downward. In theory the slope of the helix, the spiral of the flutes, should vary with the material being drilled. Quick sloping helix drills are intended for drilling soft metals and slow helix drills for brass and bronze.

The drill shank, the part which connects it to the machine, can be either straight or tapered, depending on the chuck on the brace or power drill. The cutting edges of drills are very accurately ground to ensure efficient cutting. Drills can be re-ground when they lose their cutting edge (see page 59).

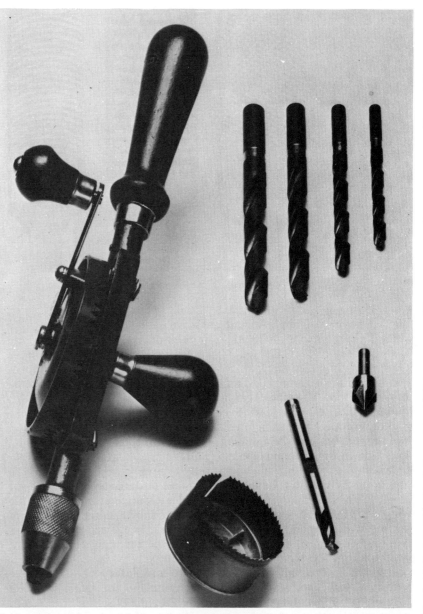

Left: A hand brace with detachable side handle. Top right: Four twist drills. Bottom right: Hole saw with pilot drill and (above) a countersunk drill

Drill size

Drill sizes are measured either in wire gauge sizes, letter sizes from A to Z, millimeters from 0.3 mm. to 100 mm., or in fractions of an inch from $\frac{1}{64}$ in. to 3 in. increasing by $\frac{1}{64}$ of an inch. Drill size can be checked with a drill gauge, a thin metal plate pierced with holes corresponding to the sizes in each scale.

Countersink drill

Countersink drills are used to shape the top of a drilled hole into a cone to take the head of a counter-sunk screw, rivet or bolt so that it can be set flush with the surface of the metal.

Drill at a slower speed than with a twist drill. Feed the countersink in slowly and drill with care. The hole must fit the screw head exactly, so check by holding the screw upside down over the hole.

Speed and feed

The speed at which a drill revolves and the feed, the distance the drill enters the metal with each rev-olution, depend on the drill size, the material being drilled, the depth of the hole being made and the use of a cutting fluid. As a general rule, the larger the drill, the slower the speed and the softer the material, the higher the speed. A cutting fluid allows you to drill at a higher speed. It cools the metal and the drill and lubricates the swarf, allowing it to move upwards freely. Some metals can be drilled dry, for example cast iron and brass, but the drill should be watched and not allowed to get too hot.

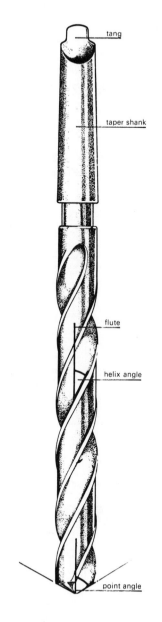

A taper-shanked twist drill with the different parts indicated

The following chart indicates cut-ting fluids appropriate to various metals.

Metal	Cutting fluid
Aluminum	Kerosene
Brass	Dry or soluble oil
Cast iron	Dry
Mild steel	Soluble oil
Carbon steel	Soluble oil

Soluble oil is sold under a variety of brand names. It forms an emul-sion when mixed with water. You can use a light, all-purpose house-hold oil instead.

How to drill

Accurate drilling needs careful preparation. First locate the drilling point by scribing two lines at right angles. The point where the lines intersect will be the center of the hole. Make a punch mark at this point with a center punch. The impression must be large enough to take the tip of the drill. If you have not positioned the punch accurately and the mark is off-center, hold the punch at an angle and re-punch the hole.

For a large hole, more than about $\frac{3}{8}$ in. (9 mm.) in diameter drill a pilot hole first. The point of a large drill bit is too large to be positioned accurately in a center punch mark. The diameter of the pilot hole should be a little larger than the point of the drill, so that the cutting edges of the large drill will be able to begin cutting with less friction. To be really accurate, scribe a circle, using dividers or a compass, which is the exact diameter of the drill and center punch the center of this circle.

Hold the point of the drill vertically over the center punch mark. Feed the drill in carefully so that it begins to cut into the punch mark. Lift the drill and check that you are drilling true. If the drill is wandering, cut a groove in the opposite direction using the punch or a diamond or half-round chisel. You can only make corrections in guiding the drill while the bit is drilling with its tip. Once it has started cutting to its full diameter no corrections can be made. Feed the

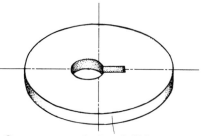

Correct a wandering drill by cutting a groove with a half round chisel

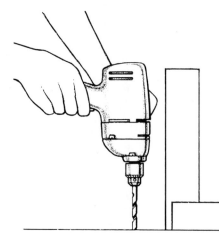

drill in with just enough pressure to make the drill cut the metal and apply the appropriate cutting fluid to facilitate cutting.

Holding metal for drilling

Always clamp metal securely before drilling. If you don't, the workpiece itself could start revolving dangerously. Never hold the metal being drilled in your hand. If the piece is small, hold it with pliers or a monkey wrench padded with paper so that the jaws do not damage the metal. Clamp larger pieces to the bench top with a piece of waste wood beneath them.

Types of drill

A hole saw is used to cut large holes in thin metal. It consists of a blade like a hacksaw blade wrapped around a body and screwed in place. It can be used at slow speed in a power drill. Always drill a pilot hole first. The sizes increase by $\frac{1}{8}$

Above: Stand a square up beside the drill to ensure that you are drilling straight.

Left: To drill through more than one piece, clamp the pieces together and drill through both at the same time

in. (3 mm.) from $\frac{5}{8}$ in. (15 mm.) to 6 in. (150 mm.).

A hand drill or wheel brace is used with drills and countersinks with parallel shanks. It is slower and more laborious than a power drill, but easier to control and cheaper to buy. It can also get into awkward corners where a power drill cannot reach. The side handle is removable and is used only when more pressure and control are needed.

Reamers

A reamer is used after the initial drilling to form an extremely accurate hole. A reamer cannot drill the hole itself, but it enlarges the hole already drilled making it round, smooth and accurate. It is impossible to drill a truly accurate and even hole using a twist drill.

You can buy hand or machine reamers. They are sized in the same way as twist drills. Machine reamers are used in a power drill at half the speed of a twist drill. Hand reamers have square shanks and are held in a tap wrench (page 65).

Reamers are tapered slightly so they can enter the hole easily. They are used with a cutting fluid and always turned in a clockwise direction, whether entering or leaving a hole.

You will only need reamers for precision work. They are expensive, high quality precision tools and must be treated with care. The edges of the long flutes can chip if they are allowed to roll against each other. Wrap each one in paper and store it in its own box.

A hand reamer. Used to finish and true up a drilled hole in precision work

Power drill

An electric power drill has a number of different uses for the metalworker—buffing, grinding, polishing and driving screws as well as drilling and countersinking.

Power drills are graded by their chuck capacity, that is, the maximum diameter of drill which will fit in the chuck. This will usually be up to $\frac{3}{8}$ in. (9 mm.) or $\frac{1}{2}$ in. (12 mm.) for ordinary power drills, larger for heavy duty commercial models. A drill with a two speed or variable power unit is a better buy than a single speed drill as it is much more flexible. The drilling speed which is measured in revolutions per minute (rpm) depends on the size of the bit and metal being drilled. The slower the rate of revolution, the more twisting power or torque is created. High speed models drill quickly through wood but they are not always powerful enough to drill through harder metals.

How to drill

Mark out and center punch the hole. The work must be very securely clamped for power drilling because the drill breaks through the metal with considerable force and can send the piece spinning. Position the drill in the pilot hole or center punch mark and then switch on. If you practice drilling a few times you will soon learn the right amount of pressure to apply. Harder materials obviously require more pressure than soft ones. The pressure should be enough to keep the drill bit cutting,

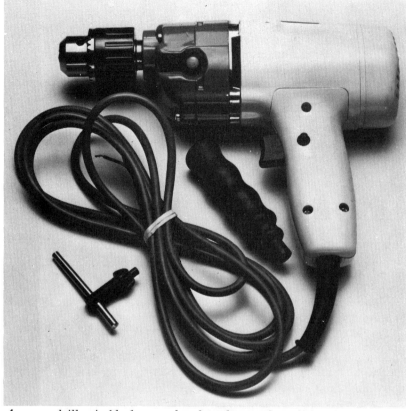

A power drill suitable for metalwork and many household jobs

but not so much that it overloads or stalls the motor. Ease up on the pressure as the drill breaks through the metal. If the speed drops and the motor pitch lowers, this is a warning sign that the motor is overloading. Remove the drill from the work immediately and run it at full speed for a few seconds.

It is essential to drill straight. Align the bit and the axis of the drill directly over the center pun-ched hole and apply pressure only in that direction. Be careful not to lean to one side, this will distort the hole and could cause a thin drill bit to break off. To help you to drill straight use a drilling jig which you can buy to fit most makes of drill. This is a metal frame which fits over the nose of the power drill and rests squarely around the drill hole. Always use a cutting fluid with a power drill to facilitate cutting.

A power drill mounted in a horizontal stand fitted with a grinding wheel

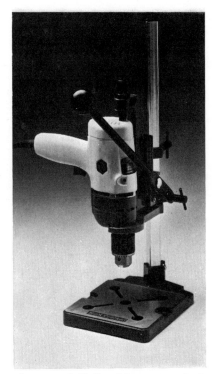

A power drill fitted into a vertical drill stand. The stand should be bolted to the workbench. The drill is lowered into the work by the handle.

Drill stands

A drill stand holds the drill securely leaving you with both hands free. It ensures really accurate drilling and is one of the most useful attachments you can buy. Stands can be horizontal or vertical. Both are bolted or clamped to the bench. The horizontal stand is most useful as a means of holding buffers, sanders and polishers, as well as drilling holes. The work is held against the head of the drill which can be set to run continuously. You can therefore have a firm grip on the work and by using an adjustable fence attachment you can work at pre-determined angles.

You can also fit a grinder to be powered by a drill in a horizontal stand.

With a vertical drill stand used to drill holes, the drill is clamped in place and then lowered into the work like a drill press. This ensures absolute accuracy and straight drilling.

Other drill attachments

Most drills can only be fitted with attachments of the same make. Brushes, polishers and grinders are the most useful attachments for metalwork. Wire brushes can be either cup shaped or the wheel type. They are used for the first stage in cleaning or polishing metal that has been heavily pitted or corroded. The wheel shaped brush should be used with the drill mounted in a horizontal holder. The cup shaped brush can be used freehand.

Buffers and polishers can be used freehand or bench mounted. The grinding wheels for tool sharpening should be used in a stand and the tool being sharpened hand held for more accuracy and control.

When you are holding metal against a bench mounted wheel, always hold it so that the wheel is turning downward toward you, not upward and away from you. Position the work on the lower side of the wheel, in this way there is no risk that the workpiece can be snatched out of your hands and flung upward dangerously. If it is caught by the wheel it will drop down safely onto the bench.

GENERAL TOOLS

Screwdrivers

A screwdriver is essential in any workshop. Screws (see page 62) are among the commonest means of fastening and there are many different types. Screwdrivers are made in different sizes and with differently shaped tips to fit different sizes and kinds of screw. They are usually made of high carbon steel with the end of the blade hardened and tempered. The handle must be securely fixed to the blade and is made either of hard molded plastic or two pieces of wood riveted to the top of the screwdriver.

Larger screwdrivers sometimes have a square shank which makes it possible to get extra leverage by using a wrench. The end is carefully ground to be flat and square and it should be kept in this condition. The most important point to ensure when choosing a screwdriver is that the blade fits the slot in the screw you are using exactly. Using a blade of the wrong size could be dangerous if it slips. If it is too small it will damage the screw slot and if it is too large it will mark your work. Ratchet screwdrivers, unless you buy the very best brand are not sturdy enough for metalwork.

The Phillips head screwdriver has a crossed, pointed blade which fits only Phillips head screws which have a crossed slot in the head. Pozidriv screws are similar and also require a special pattern of

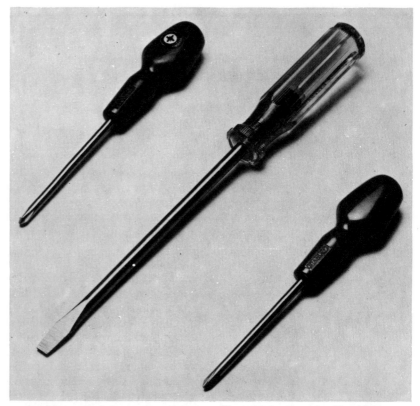

screwdriver. A right angle or offset screwdriver has blades perpendicular to the shaft, for turning screws in hard to reach corners.

An Allen key is a hexagonal shaped screwdriver with offset blade, used for turning screws with a hexagonal shaped recess in the head.

Screwdrivers, like those other useful tools, clamps and wrenches, should be acquired gradually as and when you need them until you have built up a large and versatile collection able to handle most sizes and types of screw.

From top to bottom: Pozidriv screwdriver, standard screwdriver and Phillips screwdriver

Wrenches and spanners

Wrenches and spanners, like screwdrivers, are essential and useful tools that come in a range of styles and sizes. They can be divided into fixed and adjustable types.

Fixed wrenches should fit the nut well otherwise the nut can be damaged and the wrench strained.

An open end wrench is the commonest type of wrench. Be careful when you use it not to strain the jaws.

A ring spanner or box wrench is stronger and lighter than an open ended wrench. It is very useful because it can fix a nut in a restricted space.

An adjustable wrench is a very useful tool. One or two small and medium sizes can handle a wide range of nuts and bolts. One jaw is fixed, the other can be opened or closed. It is not as strong as fixed wrenches and easy to strain if not used with care.

A monkey wrench is a sturdy, adjustable wrench, best used on square headed bolts and nuts. It can also be used for bending metal.

A pipe wrench is very similar to a monkey wrench. It is a plumbing tool, designed for tightening tubular pipes and rods.

Using wrenches

Always pull on a wrench, never push or you will not be able to control your work. Never hit a wrench with a hammer. If a nut or bolt sticks and the wrench must be struck, use a soft-faced hammer and tap lightly.

Left to right: An open end wrench, box wrench, adjustable wrench and monkey wrench

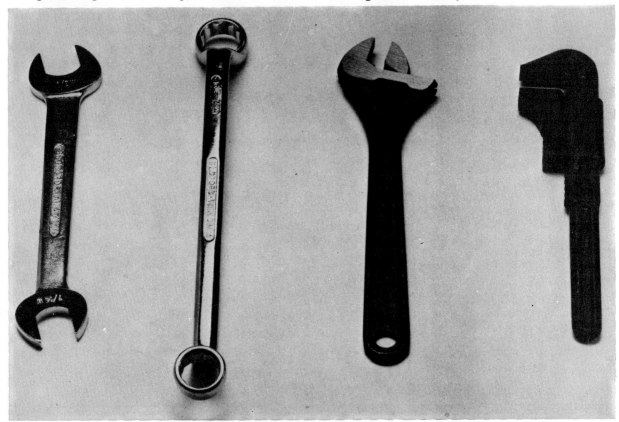

Hammers

Hammers are specified by the weight of the head and the shape of the pein. The weight can vary from 4 oz. to 4 lb. (113 gm. to 2 kg.). Above that size, the tool is classified as a sledge hammer. A hammer of about 1 lb. (0.45 kg.) is suitable for general work.

The hammer head is made of high carbon steel and the face and pein are hardened and tempered to withstand the shock of striking. The eye is left soft because it is thin walled and weak, if it were hard it would fracture under the shock of impact. The shaft is made of hickory or ash, straight grained and free of knots and is fitted to the head by means of a metal or wooden wedge.

Types of hammer

The ball pein is a general purpose hammer and should be the first you buy for metalwork. The flat face is for general work and the ball pein for riveting. On a cross pein hammer the pein is at right angles to the shaft. It is used for riveting in hard to reach corners and for making sharp bends in sheet metal. With the straight pein hammer the pein is in line with the shaft. It has the same uses as the cross pein hammer.

These are the three basic types of hammer, but many, many specialist hammers are used for different kinds of metalwork—for example blocking and planishing hammers for beating metal, and the repoussé hammer for striking engraving tools. Wooden and leather mallets

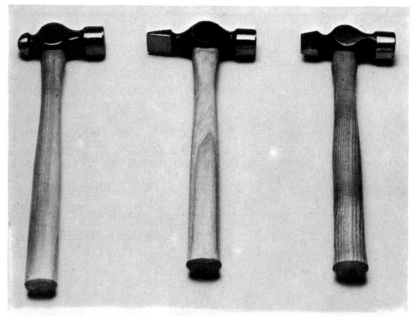

are used in metal beating, where the steel face of a regular hammer could mark and spoil the surface of the metal. Creasing and tucking hammers are used in sheet metal-work and specially shaped hammers are used for forging and shaping metal over the anvil or over special molds. These hammers will be dealt with in their separate technique sections.

Caring for hammers

Keep the face clean and free from grease and rust. At the first sign of rust spots, or otherwise as an occasional treatment, rub the hammer face lightly with emery paper. Condition the wooden handle by rubbing it liberally with linseed oil for a few minutes and then wiping off the excess. Do this at least once a year.

Left to right: The three general hammers used for metalwork, ball pein hammer, cross pein hammer and straight pein hammer

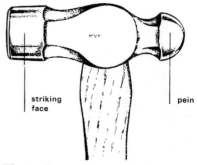

The various parts of a hammer head

striking face

pein

Scrapers

Scraping is a skilled way of giving metal a quality precision finish whereby minute amounts of metal are literally scraped from the surface. It is very easy to learn, but the real skill lies in being able to remove only the tiniest slivers each time. This takes practice but it is worth the effort if you want to do precision work or if you enjoy giving your work a perfect hand finish.

In precision work, scraping is done to make two surfaces, such as bearings, fit together accurately. The surfaces should be finished as exactly as possible first by other methods, such as filing.

First rub a surface plate, which is a precision made flat plate which you can buy, or the master surface with which the scraped surface must fit, with oil or poster paint. Then rub the surface to be scraped against the colored surface. The high spots will pick up color. Scrape very carefully, rub again and repeat the operation until both surfaces meet exactly in which case they will both be completely covered with color. You can buy special scrapers or make them very easily from old files. The common shapes are flat tapered, half-round and three-square.

How to use a scraper

The flat tapered scraper with a cutting edge on the end is used for flat surfaces. To use it correctly, keep the tool steady with your right hand while the left applies the pressure. Push the tool away from you applying even pressure and minute curls of metal will come away from the surface.

The half round scraper is used for hollow surfaces like bearings. Hold the tool as before, but draw it steadily toward you. The three-square scraper is useful for difficult angles and corners.

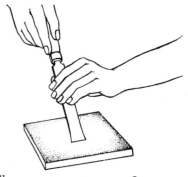

The correct way to use a flat scraper

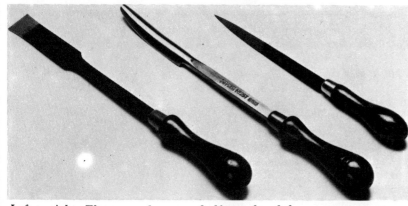

Left to right: Flat tapered scraper, half round and three-square scrapers

How to make scrapers from old files

Anneal the file by heating it bright red and allowing it to cool slowly in warm sand. When cold, file the first 2 or 3 in. (50 to 75 mm.) roughly to remove all tool marks. The remaining teeth need not be removed completely, but only enough to allow the tool to be held comfortably in the hand.

A half round file should be turned up slightly at the end and sharpened on the convex side. Then harden and temper the scraper (see page 60). To make a flat scraper, grind the end square with the sides and edges and sharpen it. Sharpen all three edges of a triangular scraper.

Scraping a curved surface

Anvil

Before you have gone very far in metalwork you will find that you need some kind of anvil. An anvil is basically a strong and stable surface that acts as a support in riveting, bending, chiseling and forming metal. The bench top or the vise are not strong enough to stand up to this heavy treatment. You need not go to the trouble and expense of buying a real smiths' anvil. Jewelers' suppliers sell small anvils, or there are two simple substitutes that you can improvise and that are ideal for the home workshop.

You can use a length of railroad track, about 12 in. (305 mm.) long as a substitute. Laid on its wide base, the track provides a rounded surface. Lay it on its side to provide a sharp edge for bending.

You can make a small anvil from an old iron, the kind with a smooth flat base, not a steam iron with vents in the base. The iron will need a wooden support. The exact shape will depend on the design of the iron but the base should be at least 1 in. (25 mm.) thick and of solid hardwood. The sides should hold the iron as securely as possible and so if necessary carve them out to form a cradle, supporting the upturned iron and holding it steady. The wood for the sides should be 1 in. (38 mm.) thick to allow for carving. Screw the sides to the base, countersinking the screws. Leave the back of the iron with some clearance as it forms a sharp lip for bending and forming

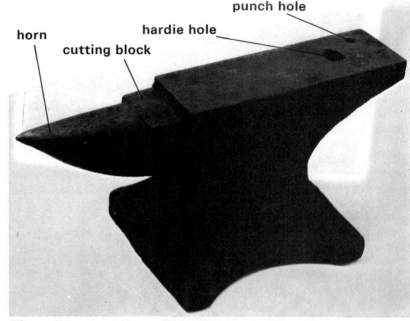

The traditional smith's anvil can weigh from 28 lb. to 5 cwt

right angles.

A smiths' anvil should stand on its own base on a solid floor, but these small improvised anvils can be placed on the bench. Be sure to place them directly over one of the legs so that the anvil has a strong support.

Smiths' anvil

Anvils are made either of cast iron, cast steel or a cast iron base with a welded steel top. They can weigh anything from 28 lb. (12.5 kg.) to 5 cwt. (250 kg.).

The cutting block forms the rest for chisel cutting and so it is left soft so that it will not damage the chisel. The horn is used for bending rings and forming circular shapes. The punch hole acts as a

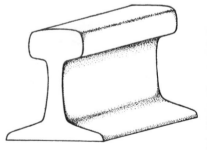

You can improvise a very sturdy anvil from a short length of railway track

clearance for punching holes in metal. A variety of different tools can be fitted into the hardie hole, stakes and formers for bending sheet metal for example.

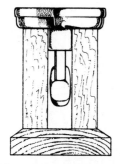

An old iron secured in a wooden support makes a useful small anvil

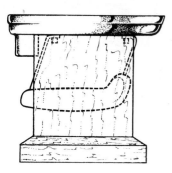

The iron used here is a traveling iron, and the support is made of hardwood

Blowtorch

You need a heat source for most metalwork—for forging, brazing and heat treating metals. There are many kinds of torches which are nowadays fueled by gas canisters. Gas fuel is clean and easy to refill, you just fit a new canister.

It costs a little more to buy a blowtorch kit than it does a single blowtorch, but the kit gives you two or three interchangeable nozzles. The flame spreader provides gentle heat over a wide area for annealing and heating parts of a solder joint. A diffuser head provides a large, evenly distributed flame, giving high heat for brazing, forging, hardening and tempering.

A soldering head consists of a finely pointed copper tip, which is positioned in the path of the flame. Use it for precision soft soldering (page 76), the tip is too small for large scale soldering.

You should also buy some fire-bricks, from a jewelers' supplier and an asbestos mat. With these you can set up your own small forge or brazing hearth as and when you need it. The firebricks reflect back the heat from the torch and so concentrate it around the metal.

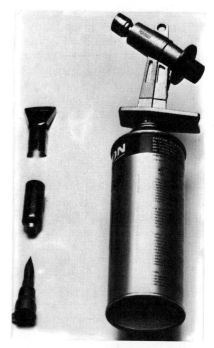

A useful and versatile blowtorch with interchangeable nozzles, (from top to bottom) flame spreader, diffuser head and soldering iron

Grinding wheel

A grinding wheel is used for removing waste metal, for sharpening tools (see page 58) and for polishing and buffing metals. The wheel can be either a power drill attachment, an integral electric unit or hand driven. The integral unit is expensive for home use, the hand driven grinder is much cheaper, although unless you get someone else to turn it for you, you will only have one hand with which to hold the material on which you are working. Probably the best buy is a power drill attachment, fitted onto a drill mounted in a horizontal stand. The integral grinder has two wheels, one coarse and one fine. Both the integral unit and the drill attachment have wheel guards, adjustable tool rest and eye shields.

Using a grinder

Set the tool rest so that it just clears the wheel by $\frac{1}{8}$ in. (3 mm.). This way the tool will not be able to catch between the rest and the wheel, a cause of most of the accidents with grinders.

Abrasive wheels are used for removing waste metal and rust, for sharpening and cleaning. Brushes and soft heads for buffing and polishing are covered on page 122.

Choose the correct grade of wheel—fine, medium or coarse grit. The size of the abrasive grain determines the fineness or coarseness of the wheel. The grit is graded by means of a series of screens or sieves. The grain size is equal to the number of holes in

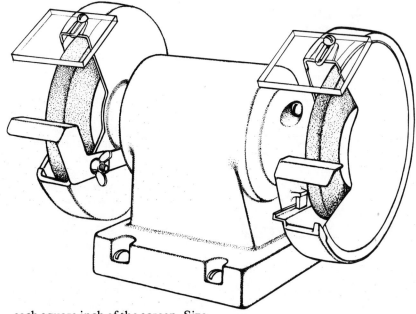

each square inch of the screen. Size 10 is very coarse, while 100 is very fine grit. For soft metals use a coarse grade such as 36 or 46. For hard, brittle metals use finer grades, 60 to 80.

Use only the face of the wheel, not the sides. Hold the workpiece firmly on the tool rest and move it back and forth. Cover other machines or move them away while you use the grinder, because the abrasive dust could easily spoil their mechanisms.

Always wear goggles, even if the grinder is fitted with an eye shield. Start the wheel running, place the workpiece on the rest and lightly press it against the wheel. Do not hold it against the wheel for too long at one time as this could cause overheating.

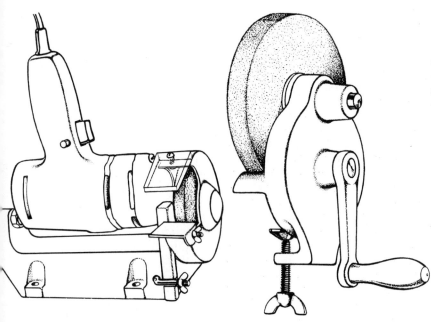

Different types of grinding wheel, (from left to right) integral bench grinder, power drill mounted in a horizontal stand and fitted with a grinding wheel attachment, and hand driven grinder

Always operate a grinding wheel at its safe speed. This is recommended by the manufacturer and indicated on a label attached to the wheel when you buy it.

Dressing a wheel

As a grinding wheel is used it becomes clogged with particles of metal, the abrasive surface is worn smooth and is no longer effective, or the wheel gets irregular wear. When this happens, the wheel must be dressed and trued. Dressing means sharpening the face of the wheel by exposing new grains; truing means straightening and balancing the wheel. Both can be done at the same time with either a star wheel dresser, or cheaper diamond tip dresser or abrasive stick.

Wear goggles and hold the dresser firmly on the tool rest. Press the dresser against the revolving wheel and move it from side to side. If many sparks fly off, press the dresser more firmly against the wheel. Continue until a new layer of grit has been exposed all over the surface of the wheel.

Grinding wheel dressers, a star wheel dresser with below it, a stick dresser and spare wheel

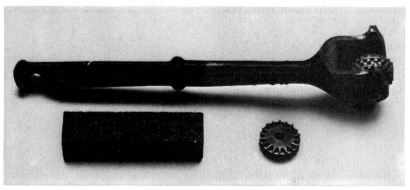

Sharpening tools

Tools blunt quickly when you are doing metalwork. Blunt tools are both dangerous and frustrating to work with so you should learn how to sharpen the basic cutting tools. Correct sharpening technique is easiest to learn if you get someone to show you how to do it. Work carefully, checking the angle frequently.

Use a fine grade grit for sharpening. Wear goggles and check that the wheel and grinding machine are in good condition. Be very careful not to grind away too much metal and not to let the tool get overheated. Do not dip it into water to cool it as the alternate heating and cooling can cause tiny hairline cracks. Allow the tool to cool naturally.

Grinding forms a burr on the underside of the blade. File this away once the tool is sharpened.

Sharpening punches

Punch points are round and so the punch should be rotated slowly against the grinding wheel. Grind only the tip and be careful not to change the diameter of the punch. Grind center punches to an included angle of 90 degrees and prick punches to an included angle of 30 degrees. The points are fragile, be careful not to burn them.

Sharpening screwdrivers

It may seem a very strange idea, to have to sharpen a screwdriver, but it really is important for safe and efficient working that the screwdriver fits into the screwhead correctly.

Screwdrivers for slotted head screws should be flat and blunt at the end and taper very slightly down to the tip. Never grind a screwdriver down to a point or a sharp edge.

Phillips head or Pozidriv screwdrivers should be dressed lightly with a file.

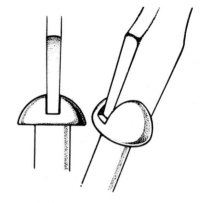

A screwdriver with squarely ground end, fitting closely into the screwhead

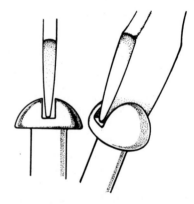

A screwdriver with pointed end fitting loosely and therefore dangerously, into the screwhead

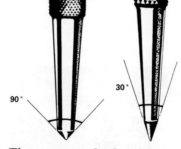

The correct angles for (left) a center punch and (right) a dot punch

Sharpening cold chisels

The cutting edge of a flat cold chisel is commonly ground at an angle of 60 degrees with the edge in a slight arc, which is the correct angle for mild steel. A cutting angle of 65 degrees is correct for cast steel and cast iron, 50 degrees for brass. The angles are less for soft metals, down to 30 degrees for zinc and aluminum.

Hold one side of the cutting edge lightly against the grinding wheel and move it from side to side in a slight arc. Grind first one side and then the other. Allow the chisel to cool frequently, it will lose its hardness if overheated.

Cross cut, round nose and diamond point chisels should be ground in a similar way. Grind them very carefully so that they keep their shapes.

The top of a chisel needs grinding occasionally too. The body is softer than the cutting edge and the head will splay or "mushroom" out after a while. This is dangerous as bits of metal could fly off and hit you.

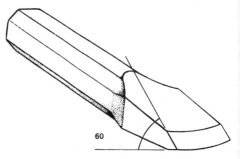

A flat cold chisel requires frequent sharpening. Grind it to the correct angle of 60°, as shown here

Sharpening twist drills

Learning to sharpen a twist drill correctly is one of the most difficult things to teach yourself. You can buy an electric drill bit sharpener, made by a power drill manufacturer. The machine can be set to grind drills of different sizes to the correct angle, you just insert the drill and switch it on.

Usually only a small amount of grinding is needed to sharpen a twist drill. Compare the worn drill with a new drill of the same size and use the new drill as a guide. The cutting edge should be at an angle of 59 degrees with the axis.

Hold the drill at this angle to the grinding wheel. Grind the cutting edge slightly then rotate the drill clockwise, at the same time swinging the shank down through an angle of about 12 degrees. Grind a little bit off each cutting edge. You can buy a drill grinding gauge which is set at the correct angle. Check the drill frequently against the gauge to ensure that the cutting edges are the same length and at the same angle.

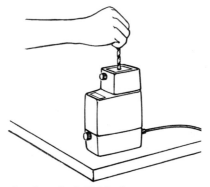

Rotate the drill as shown while holding it against the grinding wheel at the angle indicated

An electric drill bit sharpener makes sharpening twist drills almost as easy as sharpening pencils

HEAT TREATMENT

The purpose of all heat treatment is to change the properties of the metal. There are three kinds of heat treatment—hardening, tempering and annealing.

Hardening

Hardening is a process of heating and cooling steel to increase its hardness and tensile strength. You will need to do this occasionally to cutting tools which have become soft and lost their temper, or to the metal if you want to make any of your own tools. You can tell when a tool has lost its temper because it turns blue when it is being ground.

The heat treatment of steel depends on the carbon content. Mild steel therefore, cannot be hardened. As the steel is heated to the critical point, around 900°C (1650°F), a reaction takes place between the iron and carbon to form iron carbide. It is this iron carbide which causes the hardness. Quenching, suddenly cooling the steel when it is at this critical point, "freezes" the iron carbide leaving the steel very hard. Avoid overheating, this weakens the structure of the steel.

How to harden steel

Grind the cutting edge to the correct angle (see page 58). The metal must be well finished—any marks or scratches will not only be impossible to remove, they will be much more obvious after hardening.

Place firebricks or an asbestos mat around and under the metal. Keep the metal from touching this by holding it with tongs. Do not apply direct heat to cutting edges or fine points, but rather concentrate the heat on the mass of metal. When the first 1 to 2 in. (25 to 50 mm.) of the blade is cherry red, plunge it into cold water. Move the metal around, up and down so that it does not crack or warp at the waterline.

You can check for hardness by running a new file across the corner of the metal. If it is hard, the file will not bite. The hardened metal is now so hard and brittle that it will probably crack under the strain of normal working. It must now be tempered to remove the brittleness and increase the toughness.

Tempering

The hardened metal is heated gradually to a low temperature and then cooled. The correct temperature varies with the type of tool and the relative degree of hardness and toughness required by each tool's cutting edge. The higher the temperature, the softer the metal. As the metal is heated, it changes color. These color changes, caused by the oxides of iron reacting to the heat, indicate the degree of hardness the metal has reached.

How to temper steel

First clean the metal with emery paper so that you can see the colors that result from heating the metal. They will be easier to see if you are working in low light, not directly under a bright light. Heat the metal slowly, keeping the flame on the body of the metal, away from the cutting edge. Notice that the colors travel down along the blade to the tip as the temperature increases. When the tip of the blade is the correct temperature, which you can tell by the color, quench the metal in water.

To temper small tools, heat a piece of scrap metal red hot and place the tool on the metal with the tip of the tool extending beyond the edge of the metal. The temper colors will move down to the tip and you will not risk overheating the blade by using direct heat.

Temper chart

TOOL	COLOR	°F	°C
Hammer faces, scrapers,	Pale yellow	430	220
Penknife, scriber	Medium yellow	450	230
Scissors, cold chisel, center punch	Brown	460–485	240–250
Twist drill	Light purple	500	260
Screwdriver	Dark purple	575	270

Annealing

Annealing is a necessary process of softening metal and relieving the internal strain set up by cold working which makes the metal hard and brittle. To anneal a metal, it must be heated to the critical temperature and then cooled. Brass and ferrous metals are cooled slowly in air for maximum softness. However, most non-ferrous metals can be cooled suddenly by plunging them in water while they are red hot. This makes the metal about 25 per cent softer than if it had been cooled in air. You can also use a pickle solution (see page 105) to quench the metal. This will leave it clean as well as soft. But remember that the pickle will splatter as the hot metal is dropped into it and this could be dangerous, so use brass or wooden tongs to lower the metal into the acid.

Make sure that every part of the metal has reached the correct temperature, indicated by a bright or a dull red colour, before you cool it, whichever method you use. When shaping sheet metal it is always advisable to begin by annealing it to ensure that the metal is soft. When you buy metal you are often given the choice of buying it hard or already annealed. If this is possible, buy the metal in a softened state as it will save by quite a lot of preparatory work on the metal before you can begin to work with it. The categories usually used are: hard, half-hard and annealed. Check with your supplier to find out which type is available.

How to anneal ferrous metals

Heat the metal slowly until it is bright red, then allow it to cool very slowly, either by placing it in a pail of warm sand, or clamp the metal between two pieces of hot waste metal and allow it to cool in air.

How to anneal copper

Heat the metal to a dull red. Be careful not to overheat as this causes heavy black scale to form. Cool slowly in air or quench in water—copper is the exception, you can use either method.

How to anneal brass

Heat the metal to a dull red and cool slowly. Sudden cooling will cause brass to fracture.

How to anneal aluminum

Aluminum needs careful annealing because it is hard to tell when the metal has reached the correct temperature. You could easily melt the metal or burn a hole in it. To give yourself an easy temperature guide and prevent this from happening, smear chalk or soap over the aluminum before heating it. The soap will turn black and the chalk will discolor below the melting point of the metal and just above the correct annealing temperature. Cool the aluminum slowly in air.

To anneal silver

Heat the silver to a dull red, then quench it in water or pickle. If you quench it in pickle, do not use the same solution as that used for quenching copper. The acid will have a thin film of copper over the surface which will be difficult to remove from the silver.

CHAPTER FOUR
Fastening metals together

SCREWS AND SCREW THREADS

Screws and nuts and bolts are the commonest methods of fastening pieces of metal together. They are used to join parts which have to be taken apart, where more permanent methods like riveting and soldering are not practicable.

A screw joint can be made using ready-made screw components or you can cut the threads yourself. Sometimes this is the only way to get a perfect match and it is not difficult to do.

A screw thread is the spiral groove cut on the outside of a cylinder, forming screws and bolts, or on the inside of tubes for nuts and pipes. A screw thread can also be cut in a hole drilled into the body of the metal. As well as holding parts together, threads are used to transmit movement as for example in the screw thread in a vise or clamp which causes the jaws to open and close, and to make adjustments.

Parts of a screw thread

There are various technical terms for the parts of a screw thread. The crest of a thread is the prominent part, whether the thread is internal or external. The root is the base of the groove and the depth is the distance between crest and root. The major diameter is the largest diameter of the screw thread and the minor or core diameter is the smallest diameter. The pitch is the distance from a point on a thread to

a similar point on the same thread. And the lead is the distance a screw will move into a nut with one complete turn.

Types of thread

There are many different kinds of screw thread. V and square threads are most common. The V thread is best for strength, the square thread for movement. There are various systems for categorizing threads and these can be very confusing. However, you should know something about the most widely used systems, especially if you have to cut any threads yourself.

The system commonly used in the United States is known as the American National. The thread is at an angle of 60 degrees to the body of the metal and the crest and root are flat. Threads can be coarse or fine. National Coarse threads are

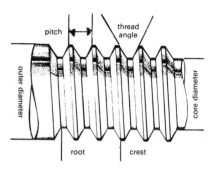

The parts of a screw thread

for general purpose work while National Fine are used for precision assembly work.

Until recently, Britain, Canada and the United States shared a common system of screw threads,

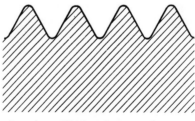

American National screw thread

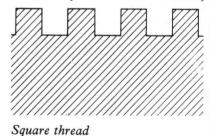

Square thread

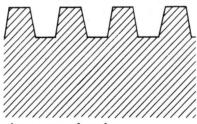

Acme screw thread

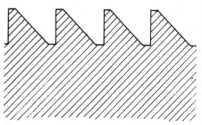

Buttress quick release thread

these Unified threads are very similar to those in the American National system and are almost interchangeable. In Britain, the Unified system together with the British Standard (or Whitworth) system is now being phased out to be replaced by the ISO (International Standards Organization) Metric system. ISO metric threads look very similar to Unified threads as they have the same profile, with an angle of 60 degrees, but they are not interchangeable because of the difference between the inch and the metric measure.

Acme threads are for heavy duty use and have an angle of 29 degrees which gives easy movement. Acme screws are used to transmit power and motion on machine tools.

Buttress threads are used when a screw has to resist a force which always operates in one direction, the thread allows a very easy movement in the opposite direction. Buttress thread screws are used for example on quick release vises.

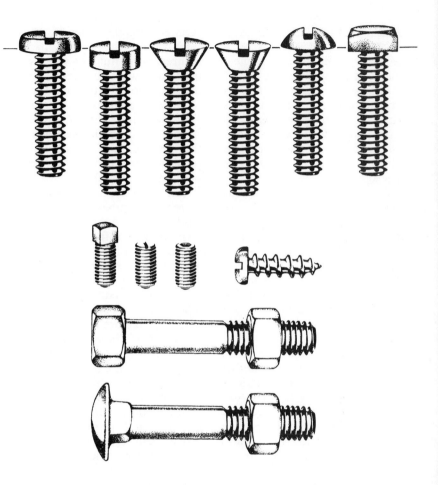

Types of screws, nuts and bolts

Bolts are usually made of steel, nuts and screws of steel or brass. They can all be given many different kinds of finish, for example chrome plating or black lacquer. These finishes are either decorative or act as a protective coating against rust.

Screws used in metalwork are known as machine screws. They have a wider thread angle than wood screws. Sizes range from 0.06 in. (1.6 mm.) to $\frac{3}{8}$ in. (9 mm.) in diameter and up to 3 in. (75 mm.) in length. Machine screws are described by the shape of their heads and by their length which is measured from the underside of the head to the tip. Countersunk screws are the exception. They are measured by their overall length from the top of the head to the tip.

Top row: Machine screws with variously shaped heads. Center: Three set screws and (right) a self tapping screw. Bottom: Hexagonal-headed machine bolt and nut and carriage bolt with square neck and nut

Screws can be used in an assembly together with nuts or on their own to join two parts, one of which has a threaded hole.

Nuts and bolts provide the most common uses for screw threads. Nuts can be square or hexagonal shaped and are internally threaded. Bolts are generally used with holes which go through the metal to the other side.

The sizes of machine bolts range from $\frac{1}{4}$ in. (6 mm.) to $\frac{1}{2}$ in. (12 mm.) in diameter and from 1 in. (25 mm.) to 6 in.(150 mm.) in length. Machine bolts have either hexagonal or square heads.

Carriage bolts are used to join wood or to join wood to metal. The square neck sinks into the wood, holding the bolt securely when the nut is tightened.

Set screws are used to fasten moving parts together so that they turn together, for example fixing a pulley to a shaft or a handle to a spindle. Set screws can have large or small square heads, but the most common type is the grub screw or socket head screw, which has no head but rather has a screwdriver slot in the top. Socket head screws can also have an octagonal recess in the head, in which case they are known as Allen screws.

Studs have a particular use. They are used to join machine parts that have to be continually separated where a bolt cannot be used, or where one part has to be joined to a softer metal part. A stud is threaded at both ends with a plain portion in between. It is screwed into the body of the assembly and the second part is secured with a nut. If a screw were used, there would be a tendency for the screw hole to strip or wear due to constant removal of the screw. However, it is much easier to replace a stud which has worn at the nut end than it would be to repair a stripped hole in the main body of the assembly.

Self tapping screws are used in increasing numbers in sheet metalwork. They are made to cut their own thread in soft metals and mild steel sheet. There are two kinds available. Standard self tapping screws have a slot cut part of the way into the end of the thread. They cut in the same way as a tap (page 65) and are driven in with a screwdriver. The second kind has a coarse tapering thread and can be pushed in with a hammer.

A washer is a thin ring of metal or rubber which is placed between a screw and a nut. It distributes pressure and protects soft materials against marking. You can buy washers or make them yourself quite easily from scraps of thin sheet metal.

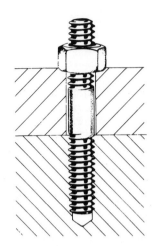

A stud, threaded at both ends, is very useful for joining two parts that have to be constantly separated. When the nut is removed, the top component can be lifted off

CUTTING THREADS BY HAND

Cutting internal threads

Cutting threads by hand requires sets of special tools. The tools for cutting internal threads are called taps. Dies are used to cut external threads. You can buy complete kits containing sets of taps in the commonest sizes together with corresponding dies, or you can buy them individually. Taps can be made of carbon steel, or harder high speed steel which costs twice as much. Individually taps are not expensive, but the cost of a set can mount up. If you think you will be cutting threads quite regularly, it may be best to invest in a small kit of taps and dies in common sizes. This will be cheaper than buying the items separately.

Taps cut a thread into a previously drilled hole. Each tap consists of a screw with three or four flutes cut down the side to provide cutting edges. They are very hard and brittle and should be used with care. Taps are used in sets of three and should always be used in the correct order.

A taper tap is the first in the set. It is tapered for two thirds of its length so that it can enter the hole easily and begin cutting the thread. It has a full thread cut on the top third of its length, so no other tap is needed if you are cutting a thread in thin sheet metal.

The second, or intermediate, tap is tapered for one third of its length and cuts a full thread with the top two thirds of its length. The third tap, called the bottoming tap, is parallel along its whole length except for a beveled lead at the tip. It is used last and should always be used when you are cutting a blind hole, that is, one that does not go right through the metal. This type of hole is more difficult to tap than a through hole and must first be drilled a little deeper than is required for the threaded portion.

A tap wrench grips the tap around its square top. It may be shaped like a T-bar with a chuck for gripping the tap. This type is suitable for smaller sizes. Tap wrenches can also be in the form of a single bar with a fixed or adjustable square hole in the center.

Sizing

The tapping size is the size of the hole which must be drilled before tapping begins. This depends on the size and type of thread being cut. It should be slightly larger than the core diameter of the screw to allow for the cutting action of the taps. It needs to be quite accurately sized, however. If you drill a hole too small, the taps have difficulty cutting the thread and are likely to break. If you drill it too large, the taps will only cut a partial thread.

Any store that sells taps will also have a set of standard tables which relate the tapping size to the appropriate size of screw and type of thread. You must remember to take things like screw size and the corresponding tapping size into account when you are designing and planning a project.

Cutting an internal thread by hand using a tap held in an adjustable tap wrench

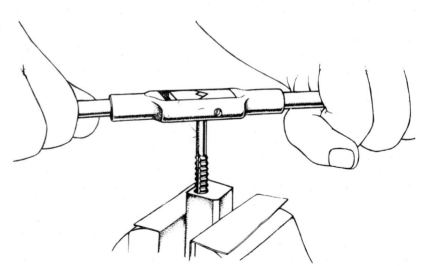

How to cut an internal thread

Mark, punch and drill the hole accurately. Fit the taper tap in the tap wrench. Hold the workpiece secure in the vise or with clamps. Then stand directly over the workpiece and hold the tap wrench firmly in both hands. Insert the tap in the hole and with a downward pressure, turn the tap in a clockwise direction, for a right-hand thread. Release the pressure as soon as the tap starts to cut, and allow it to screw itself into the hole. Check that the tap is entering the workpiece at right angles by up-ending your try square alongside it, in the same way as checking that you are drilling straight (page 46). If you fail to do this you will cut an uneven "drunken" thread that will not take the screw.

The tap is very brittle and must be used with care. Do not apply any downward pressure once the tap has started to bite. The rule is to make half a turn forward and then a quarter turn back to clear the threads of swarf. Never force a tap to turn. If it sticks, back out a little. When the taper tap has been used

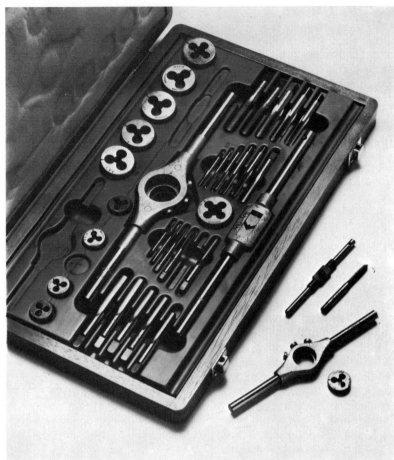

as fully as possible, back it out and use the intermediate tap.

Finish cutting the thread with the bottoming tap. If you are cutting a blind hole take great care as you near the bottom. Make sure you have drilled it a little deeper than required to allow the swarf somewhere to go. Remove the tap frequently to clear the swarf.

A complete set of taps and tap wrenches with corresponding dies and die stocks. A beautiful set of tools but only worth buying if you really do a lot of thread cutting

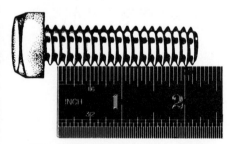

Use a rule to measure the number of threads per inch or 25 mm.

66

Broken taps

Taps are very brittle and if used carelessly they can break in the hole and may be difficult to remove. If enough of the broken tap projects from the hole, unscrew it with a pair of pliers. Alternatively, use a tap extractor. This has a square top which fits in the tap wrench and comprises three or four fingers, depending on the number of flutes on the tap. The fingers are pushed down over the flutes and tightened on the tap by screwing down a collar. You should then be able to back out the broken tap.

If this is not possible, the remedy is more drastic. The broken tap must be annealed to soften it and then drilled out. This will not be possible if the workpiece is brass or any other metal which melts at a temperature lower than the annealing temperature of the tap. You can also try breaking up the tap with a punch, but this can damage the workpiece. The best solution is to work with great care, step by step, following all the rules to ensure that this inconvenient and possibly disastrous accident does not happen.

Cutting fluid

Brass and cast iron can be tapped dry. For other metals, lubrication is important as it helps the swarf to disperse, keeps the work cool and gives the cut thread a better finish. Use a light oil or soluble oil for steel, copper and bronze. Use kerosene or soluble oil when working with aluminum.

Cutting external threads

External threads are cut with dies. There are two kinds of die and each fits into its own type of holder, called a die stock.

Adjustable circular dies are split on one side and can be adjusted slightly in size by three screws. The central screw opens the split and enlarges the die, two small grub screws on either side close the die. Dies of this type are usually used on small diameters, up to about $\frac{1}{2}$ in. (12 mm.). They are held in a circular die stock. Rectangular or two piece dies are used for larger diameter threads and fit into an adjustable rectangular die stock.

A die nut, also known as a solid re-threading die, is not used to cut threads from solid metal, but is used to true up an existing thread or clean a thread damaged by poor cutting. It is turned by a hexagonal wrench.

How to cut an external thread

Grind a slight bevel on the end of the metal rod to get the die started more easily. Clamp the metal rod securely in the vise.

The die must be fitted into the die stock in the correct way. On one side the die is slightly bell mouthed and the thread is cut away to allow the die to begin gripping the metal. This side must always be on the underside.

Place the die over the workpiece and cup your hand over the die to get it started. Apply some cutting oil in the same way as cutting for an

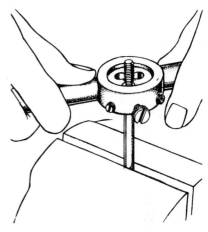

Cutting an external thread with an adjustable die held in a circular die stock

internal thread. Make about two clockwise turns of the die, for right-handed screw threads, and then one turn back. It is very important that the die stock is held absolutely horizontal so that the thread will fit at right angles to the internal thread that receives it. Once you have the cut started, hold the die stock on each side an equal distance from the die.

Dies are slightly adjustable whereas taps are not, so the hole or the nut should always be cut first and the external thread cut second.

RIVETING

Rivets and Riveting

Riveting is a way of making a permanent join in metal that has been in use for thousands of years, although in industry today it is being superseded by welding.

Rivets are short rods of malleable metal with a shaped head at one end. A riveted joint is made by pushing a rivet through a previously drilled hole and then hammering the end to swell it in the hole and make the protruding part exactly the same shape as the rivet head. On a perfectly riveted joint both sides should be identical.

Rivets can be made of mild steel, brass, copper or aluminum alloys by hot or cold forging methods. Rivet sizes are classified by the diameter of the shank, which can go up to $\frac{3}{4}$ in. (18 mm.), and by the shape of the head. Sometimes the size is indicated by the weight per 1000; for example a 10 oz. rivet indicates that 1000 rivets of that size weigh 10 oz.

The most common rivet head shapes are snap head, universal or oval head, countersunk, and flat or tinman's.

Snap head rivets have a domed head and are used for all kinds of general work where a strong joint is called for and also for situations where countersinking would weaken the metal plates being joined.

Universal head rivets are similar to snap head rivets but the domed head does not project quite as

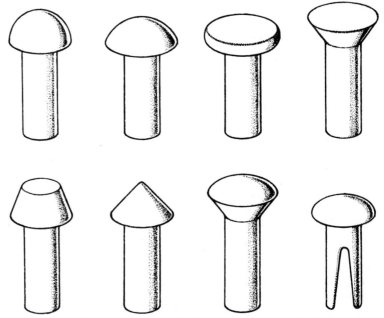

Top row: Snap head, domed head, flat head or tinman's rivet, and countersunk rivet. Bottom row: Pan head, conical, raised countersunk and bifurcated rivets

much and is wider spread making the rivet suitable for use with softer plate metals or for occasions where a high projecting head is not wanted.

Countersunk rivets are used where a flush surface is desirable. The metal plate must be thick enough to take the depth of the countersink without being weakened. You can buy countersunk rivets with a wide head and a shallow countersink depth for occasions when you need a flush surface on quite thin plate.

Tinman's rivets have flat heads and are used for work with thin

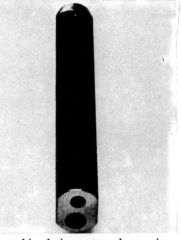

A combined rivet set and snap in one tool

plate materials and traditionally in tinsmithing. They are often galvanized which makes them useful for outdoor work.

Other types of rivet are less common, among them the pan head rivet with a raised sloping head which is used in the same way as the snap head rivet. The conical head and the raised countersunk head rivets are used for decorative work. Bifurcated rivets, as the name suggests, have a split shank. They are used on soft materials like leather and plastic.

Size and spacing of rivets

Riveting needs careful preparation. The size, length and spacing of the rivets in relation to the plate and the join must be calculated accurately before you start. Decide on the thickness of the plates to be riveted first, then decide on the best size and type of rivet to use. The dimension of the rivet shank in relation to the rivet head is standard.

First, the diameter of the rivet shank should not be less than the thickness of one plate and it should not be more than the thickness of three plates.

Second, the length of rivet required for a joint is calculated according to the amount of rivet shank required to form the rivet head on the other side of the plate. The allowance needed to form a snap head is $1\frac{1}{2}$ times the diameter of the rivet. The allowance needed to form a countersunk head is equal to the diameter of the shank. The

allowance for forming a flat head is half the diameter of the shank.

The third calculation you must make is the amount of space needed between each rivet. To do this, you must first decide on the kind of join you will have.

Rivet joints

Riveted joints can overlap, or they can be butt jointed with cover plates on one or both sides. The single lap joint is the simplest, use it where the joint will not be subjected to very much strain. A double riveted lap joint is stronger. A butt joint with one or two cover plates is even stronger. The rivets can be set in a straight line called chain riveting, or they can be staggered which is called zig zag riveting.

Spacing the rivets

If you put the rivets in too close together you weaken the metal plate but if you space them too far apart you will make a weak joint. If you put a line of rivets too near the edge of the plate, you run the risk of the plate splitting along the line. Rivets must be correctly spaced to make an efficient joint, so follow these rules: Allow twice the rivet diameter between each rivet. Allow $1\frac{1}{2}$ times the rivet diameter between the rivets and the edge of the plate.

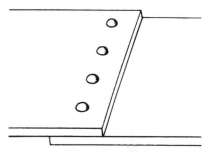

A lap joint with a single line of rivets, the simplest riveted joint of all

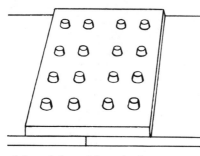

A butt joint with a single cover and chain riveting

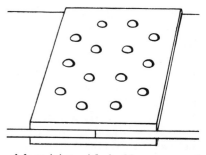

A butt joint with double covers and staggered, or zig zag, riveting

Preparation for riveting

Having made the correct calculations, cut the rivets to length. Do this by holding the waste portion of the shank in the vise and sawing through the shank. Don't cut the shank with pliers, this will distort it and make it difficult to shape. Mark out and drill or punch the holes for each rivet. The holes must be drilled or punched to exactly the same size as the rivet shank to hold the rivet firmly.

Mark the holes out on the top plate only, then clamp together all the plates required for the joint and drill through them all at the same time. This is very important. If you try to mark and drill each plate individually, you will never get the holes to line up exactly, and once you get the rivets in, the joint will be subjected to unnecessary strain which may cause the rivets themselves to shear.

File off any drilling burrs on the underside of the plates so that they make a perfect match. Countersink the holes if required. You are now ready to begin riveting.

Tools for riveting

As well as the rivets you will need a rivet set and snap, and a ball pein hammer. The rivet set is a piece of metal with a hole in it which is exactly the same diameter as the rivet shank. The snap, sometimes called the dolly, has a hole in it which is exactly the same size and depth as the rivet head. The set is fitted over the projecting rivet shank and is hit with a hammer to

Four stages in making a riveted joint

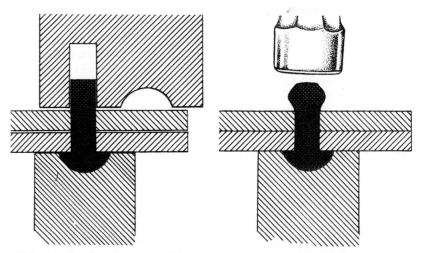

With the rivet head supported in a snap, fit the set over the rivet shank and hit it to close up the plates

Hit the rivet to swell the shank in the hole and to flatten out the top in preparation for shaping it

Shape the rivet shank into a head identical to the one on the other side, using the ball pein of the hammer

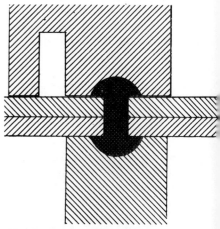

Finish off by placing the rivet snap over the partly shaped head and hammering firmly to give the head its final shape

bring the plates close together. The snap is used to give a final perfect shape to the hammered rivet shank. You can buy a combined rivet set and snap. If so, you will need a second snap or a similar shaped depression cut in a piece of hardwood to support the rivet head when the set is being used. Or you can rest the rivet head on a piece of soft metal.

How to rivet
Place the first rivet in position. Place the rivet set over the projecting shank and hit the set squarely with the flat face of the hammer. The rivet head on the other side should be supported in some way in a snap, or a wooden block or on soft metal.

Remove the set, and with the flat face of the hammer hit the top of the protruding shank so that it swells out slightly to make a tight fit in the hole and the top flattens out a little. Now shape the shank into a head identical to the head on the other side using the ball pein of the hammer. Finish shaping the head by placing the rivet snap over the roughly shaped shank and hammering down on the snap. Riveting in industry is often done with the rivets red hot. Riveting in a home workshop is done with the rivets cold, although you can anneal the rivets first if you wish and you find it makes the riveting easier.

Removing rivets
To remove raised head rivets, file or chisel off one head and punch out the rest of the rivet. To remove countersunk rivets, centerpunch the head and drill it out using a countersink drill. Punch out the rest of the rivet.

Faults in riveting

A bent rivet is caused by the hole being too large for the shank

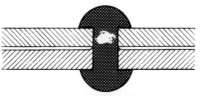

Remove drilling burrs before riveting or the plates will not meet closely

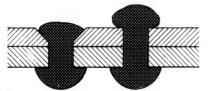

Insufficient rivet shank causes mishapen heads

If too much rivet shank is left projecting, the heads will be mishapen

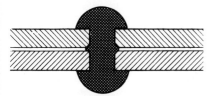

The rivet will be forced between the plates if the rivet set is not used

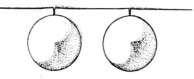

The plates may split if rivets are incorrectly spaced

Blind rivets

This neat simple method of riveting is also known as "pop riveting." You need a special blind riveting tool, which is like a large staple gun. The advantage of this form of riveting is that it is done from only one side and with a single action so it is quick and ideal for boxes, tubes or any other hollow or awkwardly shaped items. It is suitable for joining thin sheet materials, but the joint is not as strong as a conventional riveted join. The rivets themselves are available in steel, stainless steel, copper or aluminum. Blind riveting is a very useful way of joining metals together for all kinds of do-it-yourself jobs and household repairs.

How the blind riveter works

Mark and punch or drill the holes in the usual way. The blind rivet is inserted into the hole and gripped by the riveting tool which pulls a pin through from the other side of the rivet, the "blind" side. As the pin is pulled through, it meets the resistance offered by the workpiece and when it can be pulled no further, it breaks off, having expanded the rivet. The pin remains in the rivet and the shank is pulled out. Blind rivets can be removed in much the same way as conventional rivets. The rivet pin can be punched or chiselled out, or in particularly stubborn cases it may be drilled out. But support the metal on the other side if it is thin sheet.

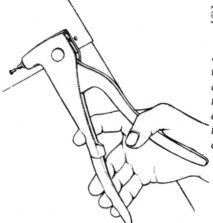

Squeezing the handle of the riveting tool causes a strong spring action which pulls the rivet pin through the hole. The rivet expands and the pin breaks off at the weak point, leaving the expanded rivet in the hole

To make a riveted joint with a blind riveter, begin by punching or drilling a hole through the metal. Insert the rivet into the hole and grip the end of the pin with the riveting tool

A section through the blind rivet and joint. The pointed end of the pin is the end gripped in the riveting tool

ADHESIVES

Adhesives are used widely in the sheet metal industry, for example in the automobile and aircraft industries for attaching sheet metal, plastic and leather to frames. They occasionally prove useful in the home workshop, mainly for fixing other materials—wood, plastic, leather—to metal. They can also be used for joining small metal parts together, providing the joint does not have to stand up to stress and strain. There are two suitable kinds of adhesive.

Contact cement

Contact cement is a rubber based adhesive. It is applied to both surfaces which are left to dry separately for 5 to 40 minutes depending on the manufacturer's instructions. Put the two pieces together accurately the first time as the glue bonds instantly and the pieces are difficult to move once they have touched. Then place a block of wood or a pad of folded newspaper over the pieces and rap the joint all over with a hammer.

When using contact cement try and make the joint, that is the glue surface, as wide as possible for maximum effect. The solvent for this adhesive is acetone or a lacquer thinner.

Epoxy cement

Epoxy cement is a very strong adhesive which can bond almost any materials together. It comes in two tubes, one of resin and one of hardener. The two must be mixed together just before they are applied to the surfaces. Epoxy cement is applied to one side of the join only. Epoxies can be applied over a smaller surface area than contact cement—an advantage because they are expensive.

Epoxy cement hardens slowly and the parts must be held together somehow while the adhesive dries. Use clamps, weights or for difficult joints try wiring the pieces together in the same way as for silver soldering (see page 80).

The adhesive can take from 8 to 48 hours to dry completely, again, depending on the manufacturer's directions. You can speed up the drying by warming the joint. Either put the whole piece in a warm oven or use a hair dryer or infra-red lamp.

Try and keep epoxy adhesives away from your skin. The adhesive can be wiped off with an appropriate solvent like acetone before it has dried.

General tips on using adhesives

Read the manufacturer's instructions carefully and follow them exactly, especially with regard to drying time and safety points.

Both pieces to be joined must be clean and grease free before any adhesive is applied. Wipe the metal over with solvent to be sure.

If you are joining metal to metal or metal to wood, roughen the surfaces to be joined lightly with a coarse file or emery paper first. This will help give the adhesive something to grip on.

The pieces to be joined should fit closely together without adhesive. The adhesive is not supposed to fill in the gaps between parts and will not hold well if this is what you try and make it do.

All glues dry better in a warm atmosphere. Don't leave glued joints to dry in a damp garage or similar place where the atmosphere is cold and damp.

CHAPTER FIVE
Soldering

Introduction

Soldering is a method of joining metals permanently by running a molten alloy, the solder, between the two pieces being joined. To allow the solder to run freely, the metal joint itself must be heated to the melting point of the solder.

There are two kinds of soldering process, soft soldering and hard soldering. Soft soldering uses a solder made of lead and tin which has a low melting point. The metal and solder are heated by a hot copper head called a soldering iron. Soft soldering is easy to learn and is quick and fairly easy to do. However the joint cannot take a lot of strain, nor can it resist high temperatures.

Hard soldering creates a much stronger joint because it uses solder with a high melting point. A much greater amount of heat is therefore used in the process. The metal is heated by the flame of a gas torch or blowtorch to bring the metal joint to the temperature necessary to melt the solder. There are two kinds of hard soldering, brazing and silver soldering.

Brazing uses a solder which is an alloy of copper and zinc. It is more difficult to do than soft soldering because of the high temperature required which must be accurately judged and maintained while soldering takes place.

Silver soldering is very similar to brazing, but there are three different grades of silver solder which is an alloy of copper, zinc and silver. Each grade melts at a different temperature. The easy grade melts at a temperature slightly lower than brazing solder. The hard grade melts at a temperature higher than that required to melt and fuse enamel powder and the medium grade melts at a temperature in between. The advantage of using the three grades is that an article can be assembled with a number of different soldered joints, using for example, medium solder for the first group of joints and easy solder for the second. In this way, the first group of joints will not melt while the second are being made.

All soldering methods require a flux. The purpose of the flux is to keep the metal clean and help the molten solder to flow over the join. However well it has been cleaned, as soon as metal is exposed to the air, an oxide film begins to form on the surface. Heating increases this process of oxidation. The oxide film prevents the solder from flowing over the metal evenly and bonding with it. It can also prevent the metal from reaching the correct temperature.

Flux does three things at the same time: it prevents oxides from forming; it helps the molten solder alloy with the heated joint and it breaks down the surface tension of the solder, enabling it to flow easily into the joint. Some acid fluxes also clean oxides from the metal. The flux used varies according to the soldering method and the type of metal being soldered.

Nearly all metals, with the exception of aluminum, can be soldered. Aluminum is difficult to solder because there is no really effective flux which prevents the formation of oxides and at the same time breaks down surface tension. This metal which is so useful and so easy to work in other ways, must be joined by a method other than soldering in the home workshop. Metals with a low melting point, such as tin and lead, cannot be hard soldered. Copper should be silver soldered with great care, as the high temperatures anneal the copper, making it very soft and easily distorted.

Points to remember

Whichever method of soldering you use, the following conditions apply:

1. The metal pieces being joined must be clean. If you ignore this point you will not achieve a successfully soldered joint. If the metal is dirty or tarnished, clean it with a proprietory metal cleaner, then wash it in hot water. If it is badly oxidized, clean it with steel wool or abrasive paper. Even if a metal looks clean, if it has been exposed to the air for any length of time, it will have an oxide coating.

2. Choose the correct solder and flux. Many fluxes and solders are sold under brand names so check the manufacturer's instructions on the container or ask your supplier.

3. The pieces to be joined must fit together well. You cannot use solder to fill a gap between badly fitting pieces of metal.

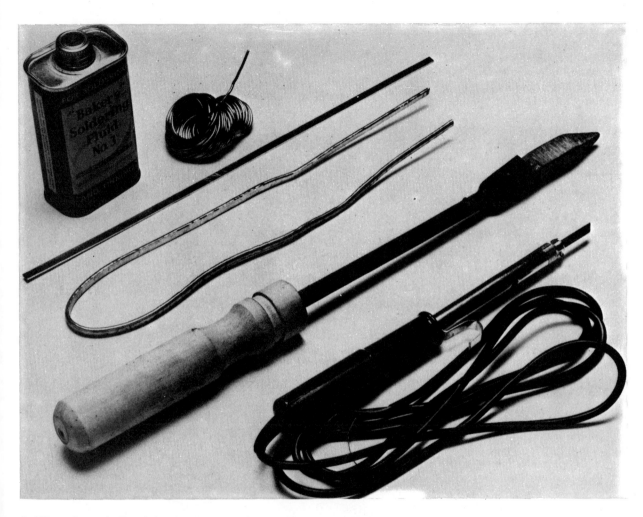

4. The pieces being joined must reach the correct temperature and be maintained at that heat while soldering takes place. This is the crucial point in soldering. The iron or blowtorch heats the metal to the point at which the surface of the metal is hot enough to melt the solder and cause it to flow, the solder itself is not melted directly by the heat source.

5. If a soldered joint is not successful, take it apart, file off the solder and start again. Do not try and patch up a poor join. The commonest reasons for a soldered join failing are dirty metal and insufficient heat.

Some of the equipment used for soldering (from back to front): Baker's fluid a liquid acid flux, resin cored solder, brazing solder, tinman's solder, a soldering iron and an electrically heated iron suitable for fine work

SOFT SOLDERING

Soldering iron
The soldering iron is the tool used to heat the metal and the solder. It consists of a wedge-shaped copper head on an iron shank. It is heated over the open flame of a gas ring or blowtorch. Alternatively, you can buy electric irons which are much easier to use as they maintain a constant heat. Soldering irons are sold by the weight of the copper bit or head which can vary from 4 to 40 ounces (113 gm. to 1.13 kg.). The size of the bit required depends on the scale of the work being done. Always use the largest bit possible for the work, because the large surface area of the bit heats the metal more efficiently than a small one.

Electric soldering irons are graded by their wattage which ranges from 25 watts for fine electronic work to 250 or even 300 for heavier work. Most blowtorches sold with interchangeable nozzles can also be fitted with a copper bit for soft soldering.

The solder
The solder is an alloy with a melting point lower than that of the metal which it joins. Sometimes antimony and bismuth are added to the basic alloy of tin and lead to make a solder with a very low melting point. The melting point of the solder depends on the proportion of tin to lead. The higher the proportion of tin, the lower the melting point. Ordinary solder,

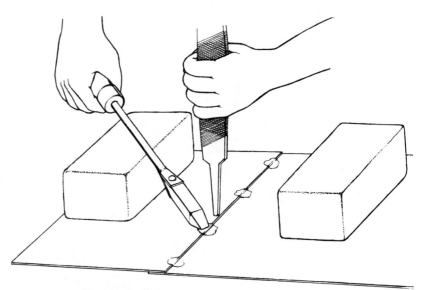

"Tack" a long seam with small pieces of solder before soldering the whole seam. You will have to improvise ways of holding the pieces together

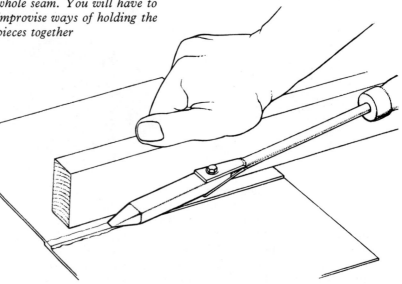

Soldering a straight seam. A piece of wood provides a good means of holding the joint tightly together

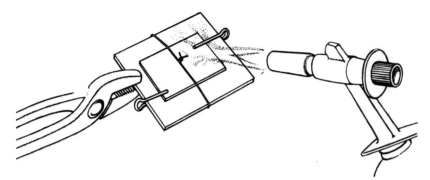

Sweat soldering two flat pieces of metal. The pieces are held together with split pins and binding wire. Notice the tongs being used to hold the metal in the flame, you should not use pliers for this as they will be ruined if they are overheated past their tempering point

A cloth or even thick gloves provide enough insulation for holding together a joint that is difficult to hold in any other way. It may be easier to tin a joint like this and then sweat it together

called half and half is 50 per cent tin and 50 per cent lead. It melts at around 420°F (216°C). Use it for general soft solder work and for soldering tinplate. Solder containing two parts of tin to one part lead is known as fine or tinman's solder. It melts at 370°F (185°C), is free flowing and best used for fine and small scale pieces of work. Plumber's solder is composed of two parts lead to one part tin. It melts at 482°F (250°C) and makes the strongest of all soft solder joints. It is used mainly for plumbing work. A solder with a very low melting point, 205°F (96°C), is called pewterer's solder and is composed of one part each tin and lead and two parts bismuth. Use it for joining lead and tin alloys.

Solder is available in various forms. The most common is as a rod or stick or as a roll of thick wire. Wire solder is also available with a flux core so that you can flux and solder in one operation. Solder and flux are also sold mixed together in a paste or paint form. Solder preforms are available at some suppliers. These are pieces of solder already cut into shape, for example, rings of different diameter. They make some soldering jobs easier and much neater.

Solder is sold in a variety of ways. In do-it-yourself stores it is often sold pre-packed under a variety of brand names. Plumbers' or trade suppliers sell it under the names given above by weight, or by the number of sticks for small amounts.

The flux

A number of different substances can serve as flux for soft soldering. You can use tallow and olive oil on certain metals. Flux for soft soldering can be divided into two groups—active or acid flux and passive or non-corrosive flux. Active fluxes are usually based on hydrochloric acid and are more effective because they clean the oxide from the metal. However, they are corrosive and should be washed off in warm water immediately after the soldered joint is completed. Acid flux should never be used on electrical joints because it will corrode the components.

Do not use sheet metal as a protective cover on the bench while soldering with acid flux. The flux will corrode the metal and dangerous particles can fly off when the metal is heated. Use a soft asbestos or plywood sheet instead. Wash your hands and any tools or parts of the workbench which have come in contact with the flux after you have been using an acid flux.

Passive fluxes are protective only, they prevent the oxide from forming on an already clean surface. Passive flux should always be used on electrical joints.

The choice of flux should vary according to the metal being joined. Like solder, flux is sold under a variety of brand names. It is available in liquid or paste form. The paste variety is easier to use because it stays in place. The table (right) lists the best flux to use with various metals.

Tinning

Whichever type of soldering iron you use, the copper bit must be cleaned and covered with a thin layer of solder before use. This process is called "tinning the bit." Rub the bit with abrasive paper to expose clean and shiny copper, then heat the bit until it glows yellow to light brown. Then either coat the bit with flux and rub it in the solder, or rub a resin cored solder over the bit. Wipe the bit with a clean cloth to remove excess solder.

A "burnt iron" is the term used to describe a bit which has been overheated and become scaled and pitted as a result. You must recondition the bit by cleaning it while it is hot with a file or an abrasive and then tinning it.

Metal surfaces must also be tinned if they are to be joined by sweat soldering (see facing page and page 146) or coated for a decorative finish (page 125). A blowtorch with a soft flame is better for this than an iron unless you can get hold of a really big iron that is capable of heating a large area of metal at once. To tin a surface, you must aim to cover it completely with the thinnest possible layer of solder. To achieve this you will need a clean rag or cloth. Clamp or fix the piece securely so you have both hands free. Flux the surface, heat it and rub the stick of solder over it with one hand while at the same time, using the cloth in the other hand, wipe away the excess solder before it can cool and harden.

Table of types of flux

METAL	FLUX
Brass, copper, tinplate, gun-metal, steel	Zinc chloride or hydrochloric acid
Lead	Tallow or resin
Zinc, galvanized iron	Dilute hydrochloric acid
Pewter	Tallow or olive oil
Electrical joints	Resin

How to soft solder

Work on a heat resistant surface like soft asbestos or firebrick. First clean the joint area of the metal. Make sure that the pieces are held close together and that they rest secure on the bench. You will have to improvise ways of holding the joint together depending on its shape. Use weights, clips or a block of wood or get someone else to hold the piece with a pair of tongs or pliers. You can also wire the pieces together (see page 80). Rivets or screws may be used first before finishing a joint or waterproofing it with solder.

You have to work quickly when soldering so lay everything out on the bench in readiness. Apply a coating of flux to the joint with a brush or cloth swab. Use the largest bit you can, have it ready tinned and heat it to the correct temperature. You can tell when the bit is hot enough by touching some solder to the point, if it melts instantly the bit is ready. Never allow the bit to become red hot.

Aim to achieve a soldered joint with a smooth, glossy surface like polished silver. If the bit is not hot enough the solder will have a dull, gritty looking surface.

A long join is best begun by "tacking" the seam at intervals with small pieces of solder. Hold the flat tapered edge of the bit against the metal and keep it there until the flux sizzles. Then put a small amount of solder directly in front of the bit. Don't put the solder directly on the soldering iron, it only makes it run.

To complete soldering, start at one end of the joint, moving the iron along the seam slowly and steadily in one direction, don't move the iron back and forth. Hold the solder behind the tip of the bit and follow the movement of the bit so that it looks as if you are pulling a thin, smooth strip of solder along the seam after the iron.

The molten solder works by first tinning the workpiece, that is covering the surface with a thin layer of solder, and then joining the tinned surfaces. If you have used an acid flux, clean the seam after it has cooled in warm water in which a little baking soda has been dissolved. This neutralizes the corrosive action of the flux. Remove any excess solder by filing it away using an old file and abrasive papers.

Sweating

Sweating is the name given to a form of soft soldering where each face of the joint is first tinned separately and then the two are brought together and heated so that the solder melts.

Clean and flux each face, then tin it. Allow the solder to cool and re-flux the faces. Hold them together using clips or small clamps and heat the piece gently with the soft flame of a blowtorch. Hold the workpiece in tongs or pliers. Use the solder sparingly for a neat join. You should be able to see only a fine, even line of solder once the sweating is complete.

Sweating is used to join large surfaces of metal, for instance to join several thicknesses into a single piece. It is also an easier way of joining awkward pieces, for example, attaching handles and feet to the body of a piece.

Taking a joint apart

To take apart a soft soldered joint, heat the area of the joint with a blowtorch. When the solder melts the pieces will either fall apart, or you can knock them apart with your hands wearing gloves or using tongs. Arrange them so that this is easy to do before you apply the heat. Immediately wipe the joint area with a cloth to remove the excess solder. If any remains, heat the metal again and wipe the solder off.

HARD SOLDERING

Brazing

You do not need an iron for brazing because the metal is heated directly by the blowtorch. The solder is an alloy of equal parts of copper and tin, producing a low melting point brass which is sometimes called spelter. Occasionally small amounts of tin or silicon are added.

The solder is sold in strip, wire or powder form. The powder can be mixed with flux and water into a paste and brushed onto the metal. The solder can be cut into small pieces and laid in position on the joint together with flux before it is heated, or the strip solder can be brought into contact with the metal after it has been heated.

The flux used for brazing is borax. You can either mix it into a paste with water yourself or buy a brand name flux in paste form.

Preparation for brazing

For a brazed joint the metal must be brought to red heat, so it cannot usually be held together with tongs, pliers or a block of wood, it requires some other method. Brazing is easiest if the joint is held together rigidly, especially if you are a beginner, so consider screwing or riveting the pieces together first. The work can also be held together with spring clips which you can make yourself from heavy gauge wire or with split pins. It can also be wired together in various ways as shown. Use iron binding wire, obtainable from jewelers' suppliers, other wires react with the hot metal, leaving a burnt mark.

In large workshops or in schools, brazing is done on a special hearth.

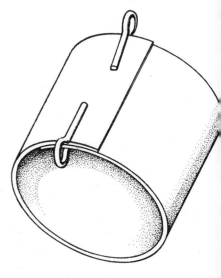

Holding metal rigidly and securely together for hard soldering calls for planning and ingenuity. Home-made iron spring clips like these often prove successful

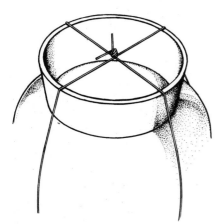

Wiring a ring to a curved base. Twist the ends together firmly with pliers

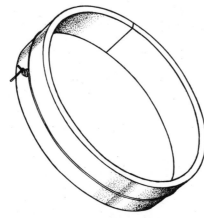

Butt joints like this are often difficult to secure for brazing and careful wiring is needed

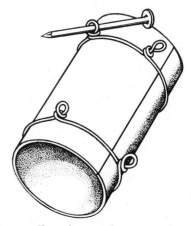

Loops allow the metal to expand as it heats up, but keep the joint together

The hearth is like a barbeque which is lined and packed with non-conductive firebricks. These conserve the heat in the brazing area, reflect it onto the work and prevent it from being dissipated into the air. A special brazing hearth is very expensive but you can quite easily build a temporary one of your own by placing firebricks, asbestos sheet, charcoal bricks or even household bricks so that you have a protective base and three sides surrounding the work.

Keep a separate hearth or protective mat for soft soldering. If even the tiniest spot of soft solder is lying on the work surface during brazing or silver soldering, it is certain to melt and can ruin the surface of the workpiece.

How to do brazing

The reason why brazing is difficult for beginners is not because special techniques or tools are involved, it is because it takes a great deal of experience and much practice with scrap pieces before you can accurately judge the correct temperature of the metal.

Prepare the joint by cleaning it and fixing it together securely. Brush it with flux and place it securely on the brazing hearth. Heat the joint to a dull red color using first the blue part of the flame to dry out the flux paste and then the tip of the inner part of the flame which is the hottest part, to heat the metal.

The joint must be heated evenly. The solder, when it melts, runs into the hottest part of the metal, so do not allow one half of the joint to become hotter than the other. If one piece of metal is thicker than the other, concentrate the heat on the thick piece. Move the flame back and forth to ensure an even distribution of heat. Try and keep the flame away from clips and any other pieces of metal which are being used to hold the joint together, as this will take the heat away from the place where it is needed.

As the metal becomes reddish brown in color, the flux will look like melted glass. If you have already placed solder in position it will begin to melt now. As the color changes into a dull red, pick up the stick of solder and place one end on the joint, holding it in the dry flux. The solder must get its heat from the hot metal, do not hold it in the flame. Keep the flame playing over the metal.

The solder should soon begin to melt and run into the joint. When this happens, it happens quickly. Remove the heat from the metal to avoid overheating.

When the soldering is complete, leave the metal to cool then remove the hard, excess flux, either by washing it in very hot water and filing off the remains, or by pickling in an acid bath (see page 106).

Silver soldering

Silver soldering is very similar to brazing. The procedure is exactly the same and the flux used is also borax. The difference lies in the solder. Silver solder is an alloy of copper, zinc and silver. It is made in three grades, each with a different melting point and composed of varying amounts of the three metals. The higher the proportion of silver the higher the melting point.

Easy solder melts at between 1140°F and 1330°F (620°C—715°C) and contains about 67 per cent silver. It is useful for hard soldering brass as it melts at a lower temperature than brazing solder and so there is less risk of the brass melting. Medium grade solder melts at around 1330°F (715°C). Hard, sometimes called enameling grade solder melts at 1440°F to 1450°F (730°C to 800°C) and contains 80 per cent silver.

The metal must be held together with wire or clips in the same way as for brazing and soldered on a brazing hearth. Hard solder is traditionally used for seams and for pieces which are to be enameled later.

You may not be able to generate sufficient heat with your equipment to use hard solder successfully and you are not likely to use this method often.

If you are building up a piece with a number of different soldered joints, use hard, medium and soft solders in that order. Allow each joint to cool between soldering. As an extra precaution, cover the previously soldered joints with a polishing compound (see page 122) to protect them from the heat.

CHAPTER SIX

Sheet metalwork

Introduction

Sheet metals that can be worked cold in a home workshop include brass, copper, aluminum, zinc, tin plate, mild steel and galvanized steel in thicknesses up to $\frac{1}{4}$ in. (6 mm.) for the softer metals. The majority of projects will call for metal quite a lot thinner than this, around $\frac{1}{16}$ in. (1.5 mm.) thick. Sheet metal techniques are very useful to know for all kinds of repair work and do-it-yourself jobs around the house and garden, as well as for metalwork projects.

The basic stages in sheet metalwork consist of setting out, that is, marking the pattern on the metal, cutting the metal, bending and folding it to shape and finally, joining the pieces together with rivets, screws, nuts and bolts, solder or adhesive. During most jobs the metal will need to be annealed at some stage to relieve the strain and hardness caused by working it.

Tools for sheet metalwork

The one special tool you must have for sheet metalwork is a soft mallet or hammer as a metal hammer would dent the thin metal. Use a wooden mallet, a special tinman's mallet with a boxwood head is best although a carpenter's beech mallet will do. Alternatively, you can use a rawhide or plastic hammer. These are often easier to buy than tinman's mallets.

There are many other specialist tools made for sheet metalwork, but you may have difficulty finding them at your usual tool suppliers. However, you can nearly always improvise with pieces of wood or metal.

Folding bars are used for making right angle bends in sheet metal. They consist of a bar or an angle iron bent around so that the two faces meet. They are held in the vise with a sheet of metal between them. The metal is hammered over the top of the bar to make the bend. This is an easy tool to improvise, either from flat or angled steel bar. The bars must be flush along their whole length.

A tucking hammer, sometimes called a creasing hammer has straight peins with sharply angled edges. It is used to finish off wired edges (page 88). Use it either by hammering directly or holding the hammer in the vise and then malleting the metal down over the pein. Once again you can improvise by making hardwood wedges and using these and a mallet to finish the edge.

A hand groover is a specialist tool that can be very useful. It is used to lock and give the final form to grooved seams (page 91) and wired edges. It is placed over one end of the seam and pushed along with the aid of the mallet to compress the seam and make it neat. Groovers are measured by the diameter of the inside curve, that is, the width of the groove. You should always use a groover that is slightly larger than the seam. Take this into account when planning the size of seams in a project so that you only have to buy one groover.

Sheet metal stakes are made in many shapes and sizes. They serve as formers for making all kinds of bends and curves. Stakes are always made in sets to fit into a firm secure base, the stake holder. This is bolted or clamped to the bench.

Some stake holders consist of a post with a hole in the top. The stakes are fitted into the hole and project to provide a horizontal work surface. Another kind of holder is the stake plate, a heavy flat plate. The stakes are T-shaped and the legs fit into holes in the plate. You can also get stakes of this kind to fit into the hardie hole of an anvil. Unless you do a lot of sheet metalwork you really need not invest in stakes. You can nearly always improvise with angle irons, bars, tubes and pipes and an anvil.

In the days before mechanized spinning, stamping and extruding processes were invented, the tinplate worker provided many essential household items

Setting out

Setting out is the term used to describe the process of marking the pattern shape and measurements onto the flat metal sheet. It can consist of nothing more than a few prick punch marks to indicate cutting lines, or for more complicated pieces it can involve accurately measured angles, lines and curves.

Setting out can be done in a number of ways. Always begin by drawing the project accurately on paper first. It is at this stage that you must decide what type of seams, folds, edges and joins you will use because you must include allowances for them on the plan.

There are a number of ways of transferring the pattern to the metal. You can mark on metal with either a pencil or a scriber or dot punch. Don't use a scriber to mark on what will be the outside of a finished project and use it carefully and lightly to mark any bend or fold lines, heavily scored metal could split along the lines when it is folded.

Methods of setting out

Cut out the pattern in thin paper and glue it to the metal with rubber cement. Either cut a simple shape out directly or scribe or draw around the paper.

Alternatively, you can paint the metal with poster paint and then transfer the pattern by placing carbon paper and then the pattern over the metal. Clip these in place and outline the design using a

A tinman's mallet, tucking hammer, stake horse and stakes. The stakes are (from top to bottom) a dish head, box head and taper head stake

pencil or stylus. Then scribe the design lightly into the metal through the paint and wash off the paint.

If you have to make a number of shapes all exactly the same, make an accurate template from thick cardboard, thin plywood or sheet metal. Place this on the metal and draw or scribe around it.

You can also measure out and mark the pattern directly on the metal. Always start by cutting or filing one edge and one end at right angles to each other. Check with a try square and then use these two

sides as reference lines and make all measurements from them.

Cutting sheet metal

Cut the metal out using snips, a hacksaw, abrafile or chisel as required. You will soon become aware of the very sharp edges on sheet metal. One of the basic processes is folding the edge over to make a safe edge. Burrs form on the edge during sawing operations. These burrs are razor sharp and can cause an unpleasant cut if you are not careful. To avoid this, always file off burrs.

BENDING SHEET METAL

Right angle bends

For accurate bending the metal must be supported on both sides right up to the bending line. Use formers to support the metal, either bending bars or two blocks of wood held securely in the vise. Use wood at least 1 in. (25 mm.) thick, it must be firm and must not bend at all when you hammer it.

It is essential that the metal be supported along the whole length of the bend on both sides. If you try and bend over a single former only, without supporting the metal on the other side, the metal will bow out into an uneven curve instead of forming a sharp, clean bend. To bend very long pieces of metal, either clamp the sheet over the edge of the bench or extend the vise jaws with two pieces of wood and clamps as shown.

To form a bend, press the metal down with one hand and ease over the metal using a soft hammer or a wooden mallet. Form the bend gradually and progressively with light blows. Work long bends over gradually along their whole length, don't form the bend fully over short lengths, this will only distort the metal and make a curved edge instead of a sharp straight one.

To bend up the sides for a box, first bend two opposite sides and then cut a wooden former the same size as the box. Clamp the former in place securely and then bend the remaining two sides up around it to make the box.

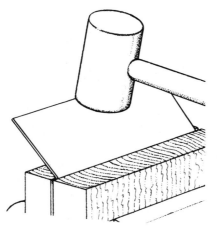

For a sharp right angle bend, clamp the metal firmly between two blocks of wood and mallet over the length of the bend

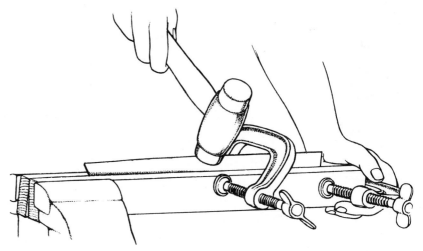

To make a long right angle bend, you can extend the vise jaws using two long battens and as many clamps as required. If necessary you can also support the end on saw horses, chair backs or boxes

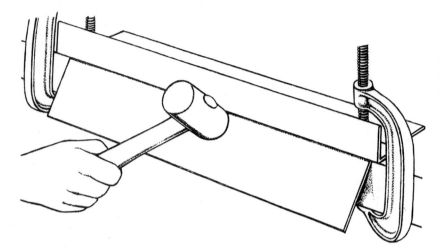

An alternative way of making a long right angle bend is over the edge of the workbench. Clamp the metal to the edge of the bench using a long batten, or as here a length of angle iron and a pair of C-clamps

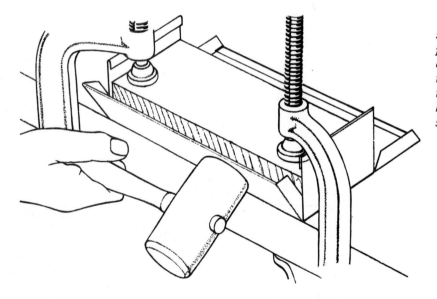

To bend up the sides for a box shape it is worth taking time to prepare a wooden former of exactly the right size. Notice that the edges have been bent over and that the bends for the lap joins have been formed first, before the sides are bent

Curved bends

Making a curved bend is rather more complicated than making a straight right angle bend. It is no more difficult to bend the metal itself but the problem lies in providing a former with the same curve as that required for the finished piece. If the former is not right, you have no way of ensuring that you will end up with a piece of metal curved to the required radius. To bend a long curve you must support the metal on the side opposite the curve as well, otherwise it will bow out instead of curving cleanly.

To bend curved shapes, cut a curved former from a block of wood and hammer the metal over it. To form cylinders and curves in thin sheet, hold a length of pipe of similar diameter in the vise and use this as a former. You can bend cone shapes in this way too.

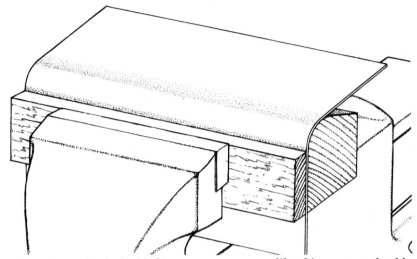

To bend any kind of odd shape or uneven curve like this one, you should make a special former. Support the wood on the other side for a clean bend

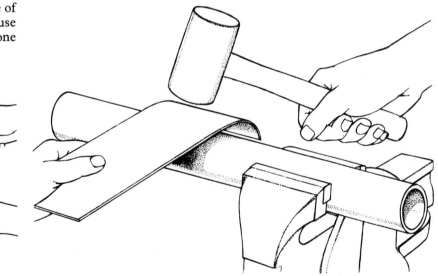

A special conical stake provides the best former for an accurate cone shape, although you can improvise

A pipe held in the vise makes an efficient stake for bending curves and one very similar to the stake being used by the elegant tinplate worker shown on page 83

Edges

Edges are formed on sheet metal for a number of reasons; for neatness, for safety and to give the edge of thin sheet more strength. An edge can be formed simply by bending the metal over on itself, or by bending it over wire for a more rounded shape. Wherever possible, edges should be formed on the flat sheet of metal before shaping bends are made.

Making a safe edge

A safe edge consists of a single bend made along the edge of the metal to form a safe, rounded edge. For accuracy, mark out the bending line using odd leg calipers. Begin by making a right angle bend. The next step is to mallet the bend over. Lay the metal flat on the bench to do this. To prevent a flat, bent back edge, insert a piece of thin waste metal into the bend and mallet over this. Then remove the metal and tuck in the edge using the edge of the mallet, the tucking hammer or a wedge and mallet.

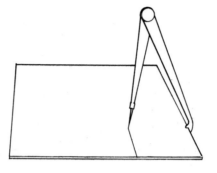

Top: Mark out the allowance for the edge with odd leg calipers

Center: Bend the edge into a right angle, insert a piece of waste in the angle and mallet the edge over

Bottom: Tuck in the edge with the edge of a tinman's mallet as here, or a tucking hammer as shown at the top of the facing page

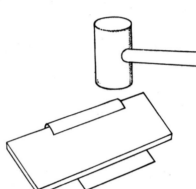

Making a wired edge

A wired edge, where a length of wire is trapped in the bend edge is stronger than the safe edge. You should use copper or galvanized wire so there is no danger of rust eventually spoiling your work.

You must calculate the allowance required for bending the metal over to make the edge accurately. The allowance for a wired edge is $2\frac{1}{2}$ times the thickness of the wire plus twice the thickness of the metal. Mark out the allowance using odd leg calipers. Bend the metal over at right angles, then lay it flat and bend it over a piece of scrap metal roughly equal in thickness to the diameter of the wire. Put the wire in place in the bend and trap it with blows from the mallet. Finish off the edge by setting it down over a sharp stake or edge.

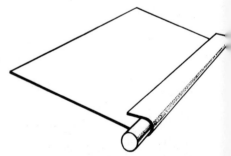

To finish a wired edge, remove the waste, and insert the wire. Remember the allowance for the edge must be calculated so that it is sufficient to bend right over the wire

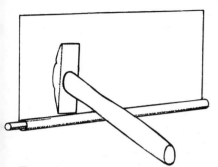

Trap the wire in the bend using a tucking hammer as shown or a mallet

Turning an edge with pliers

You can turn a wired edge using pliers instead of the usual method if the metal is thin enough. Cover the jaws of the pliers with masking tape to prevent them from marking the metal. Clearly mark out the allowance for bending. Turn up the edge slightly all around, then insert the wire and finish turning the edge. Complete the edge by hammering it down in the usual way.

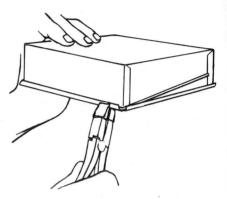

On thin sheet materials you can turn up an edge with a pair of pliers. Wrap masking tape around the jaws of the pliers so they won't mark the material

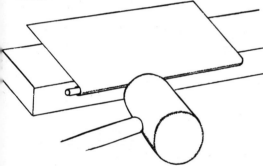

Finish off by setting it down over a sharp edge

Wired edges on boxes and cylinders

When making a wired edge on a shape like a box or cylinder, don't forget to allow the extra metal for both side joints and the edge when planning and setting out.

Always try and use a simple joint like a plain lap joint in combination with folded edges, it is by far the easiest. Fix the wire as shown so that the ends are hidden inside the channel in the edge. Remember to make the edge before forming the metal.

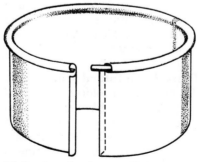

Make the edge for a cylinder before bending the cylindrical shape. Leave an allowance for a lap joint

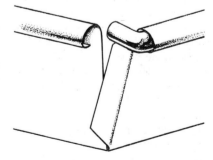

Treat box shapes in the same way. First bend the edge, then the lap joint, then bend up the sides

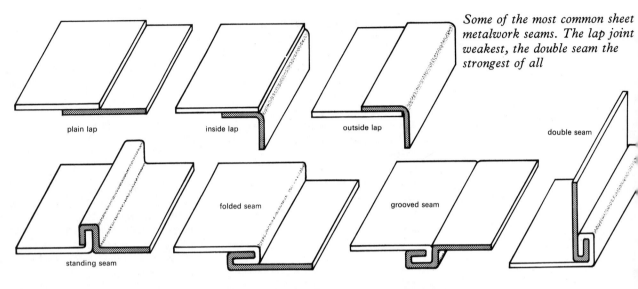

Some of the most common sheet metalwork seams. The lap joint weakest, the double seam the strongest of all

plain lap

inside lap

outside lap

double seam

standing seam

folded seam

grooved seam

Seams

Seaming is the standard way of joining sheet metal. Strong folded and grooved seams can be used on their own, but the other kinds of seam need to be secured with rivets, adhesive or solder. A seam made by any method can also be finished off by "floating" it with solder to make it waterproof. To float a joint with solder, use soft solder and flood the completed joint with solder using a blowtorch to heat the work.

The order of work when making a seam involving folding, is first to make the fold for the seam, then make any folds required to form the work, then join or lock the seam edges together.

Types of seam

To make the plain lap seam, one end is simply laid over the other and the two are riveted or soldered together. Inside or outside lap seams can be made on straight sides or on corners. They will need to be riveted, screwed or soldered to hold them together. Other seams will hold securely on their own.

To make any of the grooved and folded seams the metal is first bent over as required using the same methods as those used for bending edges. The folded edges are then locked together.

Finishing a folded seam

To finish off a folded seam, support the seam, placing it over a block of wood or over a pipe held in the vise, then mallet down the seam to lock it. If you are making a cylinder or joining one continuous piece of metal, remember to fold the edges in opposite directions so that they will lock together.

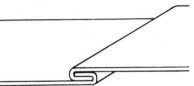

To make any of the folded seams on a cylinder or box shape, remember to make the bends for the seams in opposite directions as shown (above and below) so that the edges lock together

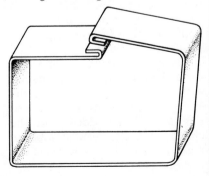

Making a double seam

The double seam is often used to fix the base to round containers. Mark out the base piece, including a seam allowance of twice the width of the finished seam. Bend up half of this allowance at right angles on a curved stake—the end of a tube or thick pipe will do. Then bend the same amount outward on the base of the cylinder. Do this over a sharp edge, such as the edge of the anvil or a folding bar.

Place the cylinder inside the bent up base. Secure the base over the cylinder by bending the vertical lap flat. To finish off, up end the cylinder over a round bar or pipe, and mallet over the seam. Float the seam with solder to make a water-tight container.

Use soft solder and a blowtorch. Secure the workpiece somehow so that you have both hands free. Flux the seam, heat the metal and touch the join with a stick of solder.

Finishing a grooved seam

To finish off a grooved seam, support the seam along its length, then mallet it very gently to close it, being careful not to nick or distort it. Then use a groover to lock the seam. The groover should be very slightly larger than the seam, by about $\frac{1}{16}$ in. (1.5 mm.). Hold the groover over one end of the seam and strike it sharply with the hammer to close the seam. Then, holding the groover at a slight angle, slide it along the seam away from you, striking it with the hammer as you go.

For a double seam, bend the cylinder outwards, 1, then bend up the base, 2

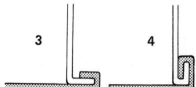

Close the seam, 3, and then turn up the edge, 4

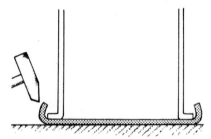

Step 2, use a hammer to close the seam on a flat surface

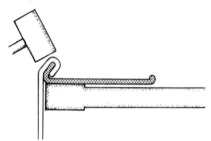

Step 4, use a mallet to bend up the base over a stake

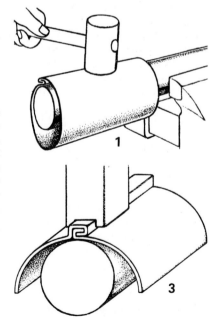

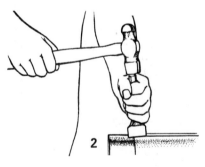

1. *Mallet the seam along its length to close it*
2. *Using the groover to lock the seam*
Notice that the groover is held at a slight angle so that the hammer pushes it along the seam
3. *A detail showing how the groover fits over the seam*

CHAPTER SEVEN
Wrought iron

Introduction

Traditionally, wrought ironwork was done by smiths who brought the iron to red or white heat in the forge and then hammered it to shape over the anvil. This is not practicable in a home workshop but you can still do wrought ironwork using rather thinner metal than that traditionally used and with a blowtorch providing the heat source. This chapter shows you how to bend and form strips, bars and rods of metal to make bends, curves, scrolls, twists and rings. These are the techniques of wrought ironwork, although of course, you can use them for any metal and for any kind of project.

Most ferrous and non-ferrous metal less than $\frac{1}{4}$ in. (6 mm.) thick can be bent cold. Mild steel and duraluminum offer more resistance to bending than softer metals like copper and aluminum. Wrought iron, which is almost pure iron with very little carbon, is malleable and easy to shape and bend. However, it is very expensive and rarely used now. Mild steel is the metal most often used for wrought ironwork today.

Non-ferrous metals should be annealed before you begin work and also during the work processes as they work harden. Mild steel and wrought iron can be worked at red heat with the aid of a blowtorch. For really sharp bends the metal must be heated red hot.

No special tools are necessary for this kind of work, beyond the range of tools that are standard in any workshop like the vise, ball pein hammer, wrenches and pliers. You will find a pair of thick protective gloves useful for holding hot metal, and possibly a pair of tongs for occasions when you cannot hold the metal in your hand. You will also need some kind of an anvil and a blowtorch. There are many kinds on the market, but a blowtorch fuelled by a disposable gas canister and with interchangeable nozzles, like the one shown on page 55, will prove most useful.

Wrought ironwork is composed of different pieces of metal which are formed into the required bends, curves and scrolls and are then joined together. This can be done either by soldering, brazing or riveting. So you will need to be able to perform one of these joining operations.

The one special tool you will find useful is a bending jig which takes much of the difficulty out of bending scrolls. You can make or improvise one quite easily if you don't want to buy one.

Making things of wrought ironwork is now a popular activity and there are kits available which are not very expensive and which include special tools for cutting, forming and joining the metal. A complete kit consists of a bending jig, a punching and shearing tool which cuts the metal strips and punches rivet holes, and finally a bending, rolling and riveting tool which rivets, forms curves, circles and bends. The last two tools are useful for other kinds of metalwork.

A blacksmith at work. The metal is brought to white heat in the forge before being bent with the help of the vise

BENDING METAL

Preparing the metal

The techniques explained here are for bending metal thicker than the sheet metal used in the bending techniques described on page 85. If you are making a complicated piece or one involving many bends, make a full size drawing of the finished piece and bend a length of soft wire over the drawing to find the length of the metal blank.

For right angle bends you must add an extra allowance of metal to make up for the metal taken up in the bend. For each right angle bend add on one half the thickness of the metal. Therefore, if you are using metal $\frac{1}{2}$ in. (12 mm.) thick, you must add an extra $\frac{1}{4}$ in. (6 mm.) onto the length of the metal blank for every right angle bend to be made.

Before you begin work, it is very important that you work out the exact order in which the bends are to be made. Mark each bending line on the metal with pencil or with a very lightly scribed line. Remember that if you scribe too heavily along a bend line, there is the possibility that the metal may split along that line. You may find it easier to plan the order of work if you make a model in cardboard and number each bend on it.

Making a right angle bend

Secure the metal vertically in the vise with the bend line at the top of the jaws. Bend the metal by striking it with the hammer near the bend line. Do not strike the metal so hard that it becomes thinned out at the bend line.

To square off the bend, place the metal horizontally in the vise, so that the edge is parallel to the top of the vise jaws. Hit the metal directly over the bend.

You can also form bends by gripping the metal with a monkey wrench while one end is secure in the vise. Using this method you can form bends with angles greater than 90 degrees. Another way of forming bends is to hold the metal on the anvil with the bending line in line with the edge of the anvil. Bend the metal over using a hammer.

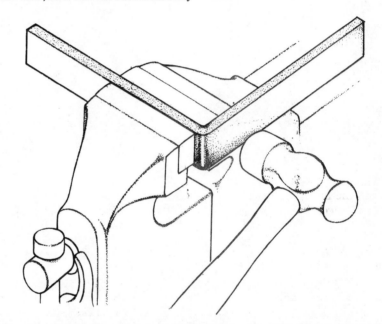

Square off the right angle by positioning the metal in the vise as shown. The top edge must be parallel with the edge of the vise jaws to keep the bend straight. Hammer the metal over the bend to square it off

Bending acute angles

To bend an acute angle, first make a right angle bend. Then squeeze the metal in the vise as shown until you reach the angle you require. Push the metal against the fixed back jaw of the vise, use the moving front jaw to hold the metal once you have pressed it into place, not to do the work of forcing it to bend. Form the bend a little at a time if the metal is thick.

Another method you can use to make an acute angle is over the anvil. Once again, begin by making a right angle bend. Hold one side of the right angle on the anvil and strike the other side with a heavy hammer until you have the angle required. Hammer near the bend line, but be careful not to thin out the metal in the area of the bend.

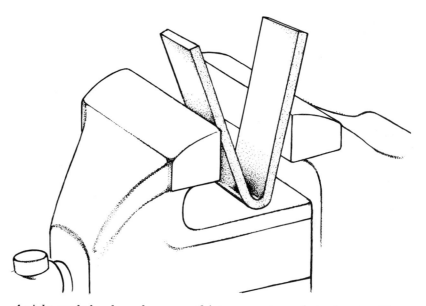

A right angle bend can be squeezed into an acute angle in the vise. You must push the metal to the angle you want, use the vise to hold it there

Upsetting

Metal distorts when it is bent because the metal on the inside of the bend is compressed, while the metal on the outside is stretched. The distortion will be much greater if the metal is bent cold. Thick metal, because there is more bulk in the bend, distorts more than thin metal. To form a really sharp bend in thick metal, new metal must be added to the area of the bend to prevent distortion. This process is called upsetting. You are most likely to use upsetting when you are bending solid bars and thick strips of metal, about $\frac{1}{2}$ in. (12 mm.) and more in thickness. It may be beyond the capacity of the home workshop however, because the metal must first be brought to white heat.

To upsett a bar in the middle, heat the metal to white heat and then quench both ends in water. To bring more metal into the area of the bend, the white hot area, either drop the metal repeatedly on its end on the floor, or hold the metal upright on the anvil and hit the end with a hammer.

The thickness of the metal will now have increased in the center, at the expense of the overall length, which will have decreased. Therefore when the bar is bent in the middle it will not distort because extra metal has been brought into the bend area.

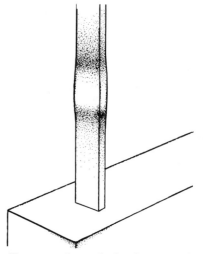

To upsett, heat the bend area and drop the metal on its end

95

Forming curves and scrolls

Make a full size drawing of each curve and scroll that you need for a project and check that you are achieving the correct curves by laying the metal against the pattern as you work.

There are two ways of forming a simple curve. A scroll is formed by continuing the curve.

Find a length of pipe or a bar with the same outside diameter as the required inside diameter of the curve. Hold the pipe horizontally in the vise and place one end of the workpiece in the vise as well. Pull the metal toward you, wearing gloves or using a monkey wrench to hold the metal if necessary. Form a slight curve, now loosen the vise jaws, feed the metal in around the pipe, tighten the vise jaws and continue pulling the metal toward you until the required curve has been formed. Each time you loosen the vise to feed the metal round, remove the metal and check the formation of the curve against the full size pattern beside you.

The second method requires the use of a hammer as well as a former. The former can be either the beak of the anvil or a pipe held horizontally in the vise. Hold one end over the curve of the former and hit the metal just beyond the curve. The hammer blows should overlap and must hit the metal at the correct point, just beyond the curve of the former so that the metal is forced into the curve. Feed the metal slowly over the former as you strike it.

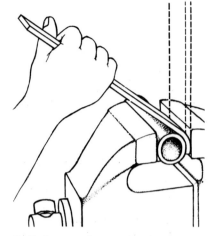

Pull the metal towards you, forming a slight curve over the pipe, feed the metal downwards and repeat

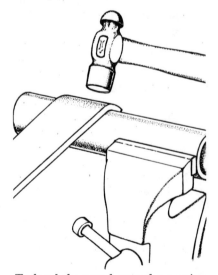

To bend the metal over the curving former, hit it just beyond the curve so that the hammer forces the metal onto the former

Bending scrolls

To complete a scroll bend you need a former or bending jig. However, a scroll is started in much the same way as a simple curve is made. It is more difficult to form a scroll accurately than a curve, so you must have a full size drawing beside you as you work. Check the scroll against the pattern frequently.

Hold the metal over the anvil, with the end extending slightly. Strike the metal with overlapping, glancing blows, moving the metal slightly after each blow. Continue in this way to form the beginning of the scroll. If the scroll is too tight, open it up by placing it over a curved former and hammering the metal while moving it in the opposite direction.

The final part of the scroll is best done on a bending jig. You can buy one like the one on page 102, or you can make your own from a metal block like the one shown. This should have a lip so that it rests on top of the vise. It need only be drilled with two holes, so leaving enough space between the pegs for a single thickness of the metal. Drill more holes if you require the jig to be adjustable to different thicknesses of metal. A very simple jig is a bending fork, made from a round bar bent into a U shape and held secure in the vise.

To use a bending jig or bending fork, slip the scroll into the jig up to the point at which the bend has already been made. Hold the straight end with one hand and

96

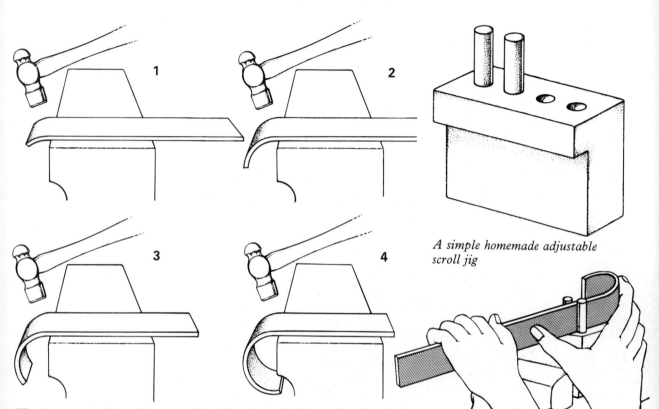

The four stages of starting a scroll or forming a ring over the edge of the anvil. Feed the metal slowly under the hammer

A simple homemade adjustable scroll jig

with the thumb and fingers of the other hand, apply pressure to the metal to force it around the pins of the jig. Bend the curve only a little at a time as you feed the metal strip into the jig.

It is always better to bend a little at a time, even if it means that when you reach the end of the metal, the curve is too loose. If this happens, repeat as much of the bending process as necessary, until the scroll matches the paper pattern exactly.

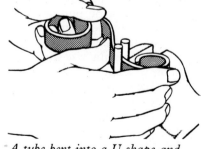

To form a scroll the pins of the jig should hold the metal snugly

A tube bent into a U shape and held in the vise makes a good scroll jig

Bending an eye

Begin bending an eye in the same way as a curve, holding the metal over a pipe in the vise. Curve the metal over the former until you have almost formed a complete circle. Now remove the former and the metal from the vise. Reverse the metal in the vise so that the top of the jaws hold the metal just below the point at which the circle closes, as shown. Keep the former in the metal. Now hammer the metal to bend the eye over so that it is formed centrally over the upright workpiece.

The former must have exactly the same outside diameter as the required inside diameter of the eye. Blacksmiths use the horn of the anvil as the former for this task. The metal is hammered over the horn in the same way as a scroll curve is formed, shown in the four-step diagram on page 97. If you have an anvil this job is much easier.

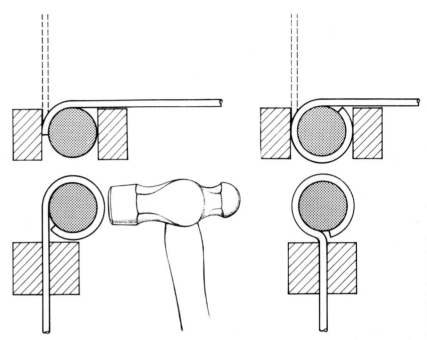

Bending an eye over a former held in the vise. The first stages are very similar to the method used to bend a curve

Bending rings

You can make rings easily from quite thick wire. Find a rod or pipe which has the same outside diameter as the inside diameter required for the rings. Secure the pipe vertically in the vise with one end of the wire also held beside it in the vise. Bend the wire around the pipe to form a coil with as many turnings as you need rings. Using a hacksaw, cut the coil of wire along the length of the rod. You now have a number of open rings which are useful for many jobs.

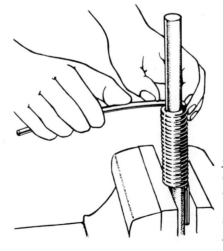

You can make as many rings as you need by this method. When the coil contains all the rings required, saw through all the coils along the length of the pipe. The rings can be soldered or brazed together, or pushed close with pliers

Making a twist

Lengths of twisted metal are characteristic of wrought iron-work. Before you begin, remember that the metal decreases in length as it is twisted. You can check by how much by making a single twist in a length of scrap metal. There are two ways of forming a twist.

Use the first method for metal that is not too thick. First you must make a simple wrench from a strip of the same metal. Drill or punch a slot in the center of the strip so that it fits over the metal being twisted. On the piece to be twisted, make a series of marks each about 1½ in. (38 mm.) apart. These indicate the length of each twist, so adjust them to suit your design, after practicing on a scrap length.

Hold the metal vertically in the vise with the lowest mark level with the top of the vise jaws. Slip the homemade wrench over the metal and hold it level with the second mark. Keeping the wrench horizontal and level and using the force of both arms equally, turn the wrench through 180 degrees. Move the wrench up to the third mark and again twist it through 180 degrees. Continue until you have twisted the required length of metal.

The second method of making a twist is used for longer or thicker pieces that cannot be twisted by the simple method. Make a mark at the beginning and at the end of the section to be twisted. Hold the metal horizontally in the vise with the mark at the beginning of the

twist level with the vise jaws. Hold the metal at the other end of the twist with a monkey wrench. Hold one hand over the jaws of the wrench to steady them and begin twisting the metal. You can slip a length of pipe over the metal to prevent a long length from being bent out of line.

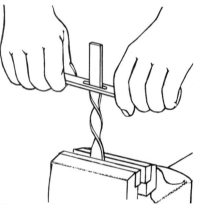

You can make your own simple wrench to twist thin metal

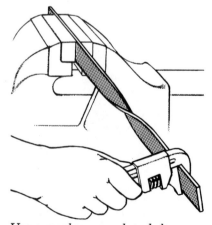

Use a monkey wrench to help you twist thicker lengths of metal

Bending tubes

Narrow or thin walled tubes are not difficult to bend. The problem with bending tubes is the tendency of the metal to kink and flatten at the point of the bend. To counteract this the tube must be supported from the inside at the point of the bend. You can either fill the tube with sand or use a bending spring to do this.

Fill the tube with wet sand and plug the ends with solder or putty so that the sand is not forced out by pressure when the pipe is bent. Bending springs consist simply of a coiled spring. They are made in various diameters to fit inside standard sizes of plumbers' copper pipe. To use a bending spring, push the spring inside the pipe up to the point of the bend. Remove the spring by rotating it.

If you are unable to bend the tube between your two hands, fasten one end of the tube in the vise, find a length of tubing with a larger diameter than the piece being bent so that the large tube fits over the top of the tube being bent. Pull on the large tube and the extra leverage this provides should make it easier to bend the tube.

If you have to do a lot of bending, you may be able to rent a bending machine. These are expensive to buy but are often available for rent from plumbers' suppliers. The bending machine consists of a wooden former with a groove cut in the curved side. The groove should be the same as the external diameter of the pipe.

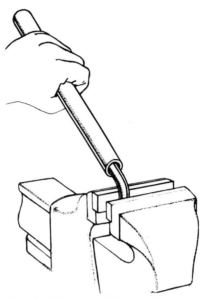

To provide extra leverage for bending quite thin tube, use a length of pipe as shown here

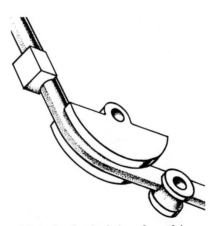

A length of tube being shaped in the pipe bending machine. These machines are worth renting if you will be doing a lot of bending

Using a kit for wrought ironwork

It is possible to do wrought iron-work and all the forming operations shown on the previous pages, as well as riveting, cutting and punching without any of the traditional metalworking tools and techniques, even without a workshop. All you need is a kit consisting of three ingenious tools and you can do wrought ironwork on the kitchen table. The tools, shown here and on the next two pages, consist of one machine with a guillotine action that cuts metal strip and also punches holes for pre-sized rivets, a second machine that bends metal strip to any angle up to 90 degrees, fixes and rivets and also forms curves and circles. Finally, there is a scroll former.

The manufacturers provide mild steel strip, rivets, design ideas and accessories like rosettes, light fittings and candle holders. The kits are manufactured to work with three grades of metal so you can use metal from $\frac{1}{2}$ in. wide by 14 SWG and BS gauge thick (12 mm. by 2 mm.) up to 1 in. wide by $\frac{3}{16}$ in. thick (25 mm. by 15 mm.), depending on the capacity of your machines.

The tools must be fixed securely to a stable surface. They should either be screwed to the top of the workbench, or for greater convenience, screw them permanently to sturdy boards of thick wood. When the machines are in use clamp the boards to the work-surface.

The punch and shearing machine. There should be enough room on each side to allow the handle to move through 180°

Using the guillotine to shear through a strip of mild steel. Insert the strip with the handle raised, pull the handle down firmly and evenly to shear off the metal at the required point

Punching a hole in a scroll in preparation for riveting. Form all the parts before you punch any holes. The action of the machine is the same as that used for shearing. Pull the handle downwards

Left: The scroll former requires plenty of clearance on all sides. The large roller is fixed off center so that you can adjust the gap between the two rollers to hold the metal securely

Left: Fit the end of the strip between the rollers, keep the metal flat and tight against the raised former scroll as you pull it towards you

Above: To make a number of identical scrolls, mark the former at the end of the first scroll. Stop forming all the scrolls when you reach this point

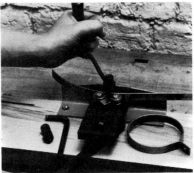

Left: This tool rivets, forms sharp bends and also rolls curves and circles

Above: Roll a curve or circle by turning the removeable handle at the back. Pressure on the front handle controls the radius of the curve

Left: To form a bend of any angle up to 90°, fit the strip between the square post and the two rollers, pull the handle to the left to form the bend. Set the adjusting screw at the front to control the angle of the bend

Above: Pull the handle to the left to bring the riveting posts together to spread the rivet

CHAPTER EIGHT
Beaten metalwork

Introduction

Beaten metalwork is a process of forming sheet metal by hammering it into shape. Hollow shapes, for example, bowls, trays, plates, dishes and spoons are made by beaten metalwork processes. There are different methods of working; the metal can either be beaten down into a hollow former, by processes called hollowing and sinking, or the metal can be hammered into shape over a stake, called raising.

The techniques can also be combined, for example, work on a flat blank often begins with hollowing a slight curve and then continues with raising as the shape deepens. This is the case with the bowl which is shown being made in step by step photographs on pages 113 to 117.

Non-ferrous sheet metal $\frac{1}{32}$ in. (0.80 mm.) to $\frac{1}{16}$ in. (1.5 mm.) thick is most commonly used for beaten metalwork—copper, brass, gilding metal, nickel silver, pewter, aluminum, silver and gold can all be shaped by hammering.

Use copper for your first beaten metalwork projects as it is by far the easiest metal to work. Gilding metal is also quite easy to work in this way and it has a very attractive golden color when polished. Brass and nickel silver are rather harder metals while pewter, gold and silver are too expensive to work without experience. Work with the softer, less expensive metals first and you will acquire a feeling for the way cold metal behaves under the blows of the hammer before you move onto hard or expensive metals. Raising, the traditional silversmith's way of forming vessels of all kinds is more difficult than hollowing or sinking and requires a lot of practice and skill.

Each method of beaten metalwork calls for the use of different, specially shaped hammers or mallets and formers or stakes. However, certain preparations are common to all these techniques.

Preparations for beaten metalwork

First, always begin with a drawing of the object you are making. The drawing should show the project in cross section and must be the same size as the finished article. You should be completely satisfied with the shape you have designed before you begin work on the metal. Only the most experienced workers are able to develop designs as they work without using a drawing.

Second, you must estimate the size of the blank to be cut from the sheet metal, so that this flat piece when hammered will result in a piece of the required size.

Next the metal must be annealed so that you begin work with the material as soft as possible. Annealing causes oxides to form on the surface of the metal. Before proceeding to work the metal the oxides must be removed by soaking the metal in an acid bath in a process called pickling. After pickling the metal is washed and if necessary, scrubbed with pumice powder and then dried. This process of annealing, pickling, washing and drying must be repeated often during the working process whenever the metal becomes work hardened. You can tell when this happens because the metal begins to feel springy and hard, it makes a duller sounding noise as the hammer strikes it.

The finishing processes are common to the different methods of beaten metalwork. Planishing is done when the shaping process is complete. It consists of even hammering all over the metal to improve its surface. The edge of the beaten piece must be made true and the surface is then given its final finishing treatment, whether this is polishing, painting or lacquering.

Estimating the size of a blank

The blank cut from sheet metal should be about 20 to 30 per cent larger than the finished piece. You must therefore have an accurate, full-size sectional drawing to work out the size of the blank. There are a number of ways of estimating size.

1. Lay a piece of wire over the drawing, bending it to the exact shape of the cross section. By straightening it out you can determine the diameter, width or length of the piece you are making.

2. Estimate the size of the blank by the method shown in the diagram. Take the full size drawing and a pair of compasses and place the compasses on the center of the item at A and on the edge of B. Draw an arc to the horizontal. Repeat for the other side. This will give you the diameter of the blank.

3. For deep vessels, double the height measurement and add it to the diameter of the base.

4. Step off the cross section with a pair of dividers.

Cutting and preparing the metal

Mark out the shape of the blank using a scriber or a pencil. Cut out the blank, removing any unevenness on the edge with a file. If you hold the metal in a vise to cut it, use soft fiber vise jaws or pad the jaws with paper to protect the metal. From now on you must take great care to keep the metal free of scratches and blemishes of any kind or these will appear on your

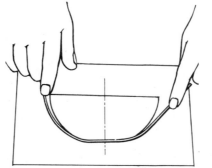

To estimate the size of blank required, lay a piece of flexible wire over a cross section drawing of the project

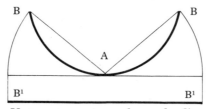

Use compasses to work out the diameter of the blank. With the point at A draw an arc from B to B¹

finished piece. Remove scratches by bending the metal so that the scratch is accessible to a fine file. Remove any file marks by rubbing the metal with a polishing stone (see page 121).

It is important that the metal and the hammers and stakes used for beaten metalwork are absolutely clean, shiny and free of scratches, grit, dirt and blemishes of any kind. If you beat dirty metal, small particles of oxide or grit are transferred from the metal to the hammer or stake and their impression transferred onto the metal with

every hammer blow. The same applies to rust. Always rub a light coating of grease over the working surface of these special tools before you put them away to prevent rust from forming. Keep hammer and stake faces shiny by polishing them with a polishing compound (see page 122).

Pickling

Pickling solution can be made from a number of different acids, but it is most commonly made up of 1 part sulphuric acid and 8 parts water. You can buy sulphuric acid from your pharmacist. A 30 per cent solution of hydrochloric acid, sometimes sold in hardware stores as Spirit of Salts, can be mixed with one part acid to two parts water and used as a pickle. Jeweler's suppliers sell a special dry pickle mixture in powder form. If you can buy this, do so, as it is much safer to use than acid. Follow the manufacturers' instructions for its use exactly.

If you make up an acid solution, keep it in an earthenware or glass container large enough to hold your largest project easily. The container must have a cover and the acid must be stored in a well ventilated place away from your tools because the fumes from the acid rust iron and steel very quickly.

When mixing the pickle solution, always add acid to the water, *never* the other way around. Stir it with a glass rod or wooden stick. Never dip very hot metal in the pickle solution, it will cause the acid to spit.

After annealing, allow the metal to cool until it is only slightly warm. Hold the workpiece in brass or wooden tongs and slide it into the acid bath, don't drop it in or the acid will splash. Leave the workpiece in the acid for 5 to 10 minutes, then remove it and rinse it

Tools for hollowing and sinking. Left to right: A blocking hammer, two bossing mallets and a leather sandbag

under warm running water.

Safety points

Follow the procedure outlined above. Always work in a well ventilated area. Keep the acid solution away from tools and safely away from children and animals. Always try and keep the acid away from skin and clothing.

Bicarbonate of soda neutralizes the acid so always keep some nearby when using pickle.

Be very careful. If you get acid on your skin, wash it off immediately with running water and neutralize with bicarbonate of soda.

If you splash any acid in your eye, hold your head under running water and let it wash over your eye. Then consult a doctor as soon as

possible. If acid spills on your clothes, neutralize with bicarbonate of soda and rinse in several changes of water.

Hollowing

Hollowing is the simplest of all the beaten metalwork processes and is a good way for beginners to start learning the process. It is used to make shallow shapes like dishes, trays, bowls and spoons. The metal is stretched during the process, so if the shape were too deep the metal would be made thin and weak and could split. The depth of a hollowed vessel should, as a general rule, not be more than one third of its diameter.

The tools used in hollowing are either a wooden bossing mallet or a blocking hammer. The mallet has a pear shaped head, and the blocking hammer, also called a hollowing hammer, has a long head with two ball peins, usually of different sizes. The mallet with its large head is best for beginners, the hammer's smaller head is best for forming vessels with small diameter.

You will also need a former of some kind on which to shape the work. This can be either a sandbag or a hollow in a block of solid wood. Make a sandbag from two circles of canvas or leather stitched together firmly and filled with sand, you can also buy sandbags from a good jewelers' supplier. However, sandbags can split and the size and shape of the hollow varies with the weight and placing of each hammer blow, so it is not as good as a rigid former.

You can make a rigid former from a block of solid hardwood, but this is in itself not a very easy

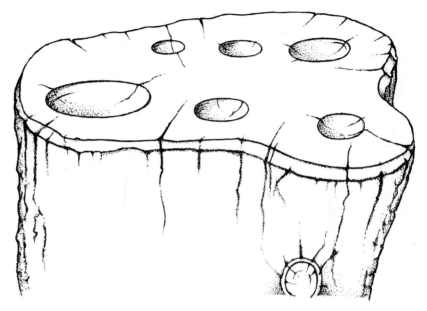

job. Beech wood is best. Clamp the block to the workbench and gouge out a hollow from the endgrain, or if you can, get someone with a lathe to turn a hollow into the endgrain. The hollow need not be the exact shape of your bowl, but it must have the same curve. Save the hardwood former to use on future work. You cannot buy a wooden former. Craftsmen always make their own, either from blocks of wood which are convenient to use as they can be held in the vise, or from a length of tree trunk with a hollow gouged out of the end. The tree trunk, commonly beech or elm, should be the right height to act as a work surface. A number of hollows of different shapes and sizes can be gouged out as and when you need them.

Above: A tree trunk former
Below: Stages in hollowing a simple bowl shape

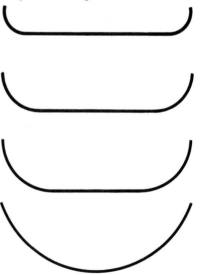

How to form metal by hollowing

Hold the metal on the former and begin striking it a little way in from the outside edge. Work around the edge as you slowly rotate the metal so that the hammer or mallet is always hitting the former in the same place. Begin a second course of blows inside the first and continue in this way, working in toward the center. To help you to work in even, concentric circles, draw a series of concentric circles $\frac{1}{2}$ in. (12 mm.) apart on the metal using a pencil and compass which will give you a pattern to follow.

Do not allow any creases or crinkles to form in the edge of the blank as the curve begins to form. If you are hammering down into a solid former, as with raising and forgework, the object is to hit the metal just beyond the edge of the former so that the metal is forced into the shape. If you are using a sandbag, even more skill and judgement is called for to create a smooth, even shape, so do try to learn the process using a solid former. Be careful not to thin the metal out so much that it splits.

Anneal, pickle and clean the workpiece as soon as the metal hardens. Redraw the pencil circles and continue working around the bowl until its curves fit the curve of the former evenly with no bulges. It is important to take your time and work carefully to get the curve of the metal even and smooth. Finish off by planishing the metal all over as shown on page 118.

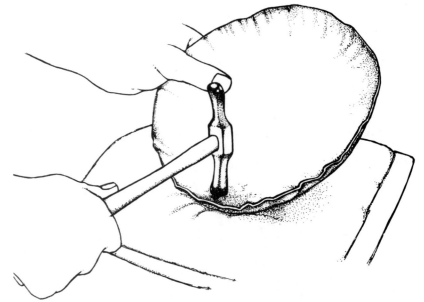

Hollowing a bowl shape using a blocking hammer with a sandbag former. Rotate the metal and always hit the former in the same place

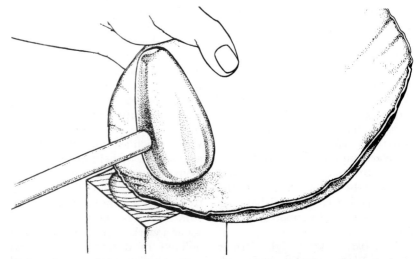

Using the rounded end of a bossing mallet to shape a piece of metal over a solid wooden former gouged in the end grain of a wood block

Sinking

Sinking is a similar process to hollowing, except that only part of the blank is shaped, leaving a flat rim, and a flat base, like a plate.

There is often confusion over the different terms for these two processes. Hollowing is sometimes referred to as sinking, sinking is sometimes known as dishing, and both processes are occasionally called "beating down".

Use the bossing mallet or blocking hammer for beating the metal. You must make a wooden former to fit the curve you want, like the one shown. Use hardwood for the body and dowel pegs or pins to act as stops so that the rim is a constant size. The blank is hammered to the shape of the curve, the dowel stops ensuring that the flat rim and the curve are kept constant.

How to form metal by sinking

Prepare the blank and hold it firmly against the dowel stops. Strike the metal just beyond the edge of the former block. Rotate the metal slightly after each stroke, working around the piece. The difficult part with sinking is that the rim must be kept flat. Do this by hitting the metal with a flat-faced mallet against a flat surface. Anneal and clean the metal frequently. Flatten the base of the workpiece towards the end of the work. It needs careful work to ensure that the rim and the base are both flattened without the curve being distorted.

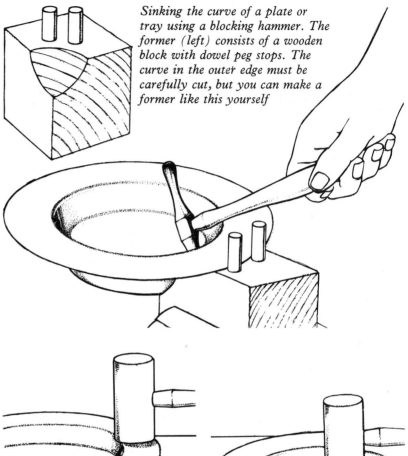

Sinking the curve of a plate or tray using a blocking hammer. The former (left) consists of a wooden block with dowel peg stops. The curve in the outer edge must be carefully cut, but you can make a former like this yourself

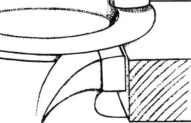

Truing up the rim towards the end of the work. Rim and base must be kept flat without distorting the curve

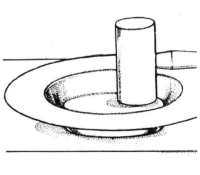

Flattening the base. You can use a flat faced mallet as shown or a tray setting hammer which is flat faced and heavy

109

Raising

Raising takes more practice and patience to work successfully than hollowing or sinking, but it is well worth the effort. It is done from the outside of the blank, working from the center outwards against a hard metal support. You can begin raising with a flat blank, or you can form a slight curve first by hollowing. Try both methods and use whichever you prefer. The process literally causes the metal to move and flow under the hammer and to contract and thicken, unlike hollowing and sinking which stretch the metal making it thinner. You can make any shape this way.

The tools used are a wedge shaped raising mallet, which you can carve yourself from a round tinman's mallet, or a raising hammer. The raising hammer has flat faces with slightly rounded corners. The mallet is slower and less accurate than the hammer, but it is easier for beginners to handle. You also need a stake, or better still, a selection of stakes of different shapes and sizes. The stake is smooth and highly polished on its working surface.

If possible, try and learn this process by watching an experienced craftsman at work. A series of photographs starting on page 113 show a simple bowl shape being raised. Another advantage of learning from a person rather than a book is that you will be able to try out hammers of different weights and sizes to find your best way of working.

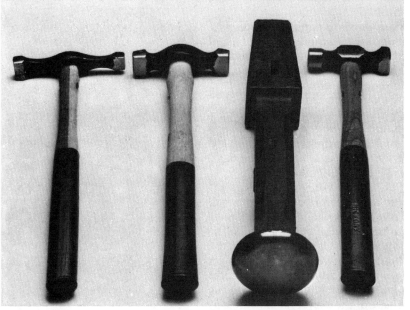

Tools for raising. From left to right: Raising hammer, planishing hammer, a planishing stake which can be held either in the vise or in a stake horse, and a collet hammer

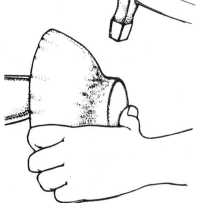

Raising a bowl shape on the arm of a raising stake using a raising hammer. Notice that the base is being kept flat

110

How to form metal by raising

Prepare the blank and draw a series of concentric circles on it. Hold the blank on the stake at an angle and start striking the metal from the center, working outward in concentric circles to the edge. This process is called coursing. The metal must be annealed after each course is completed. Redraw the concentric circles after each annealing.

Hit the metal just above the point where it is in contact with the stake so that the action forces the metal onto the stake. You must hold the work firmly so that it is not displaced by the hammer blows. It is most important that you hold the metal on the stake in the right way and that you hit it in the right place. If you hit the metal where it touches the stake, the metal will be trapped between the two and stretched thin, not shaped onto the stake as it should be. The metal will tend to crinkle vertically toward the top as you work up to the edge. Try and keep this tendency to a minimum. Do not try and remove crinkles by hammering a fold into the metal, and beware of doing this by accident. As you near the top, work with great care to ensure that you are working toward the shape you want, and that you do not bend a fold or cause a split in the metal where it has become thin or stretched. If the metal should split it is possible to repair it by silver soldering it together, but this is not satisfactory and you will have to work very carefully over the solder.

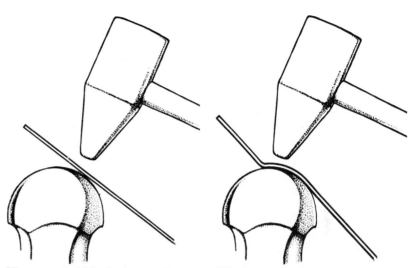

You must hold both the metal on the stake and the raising mallet or hammer at the correct angle

Hit the metal just beyond its point of contact with the stake so that it is forced onto the stake

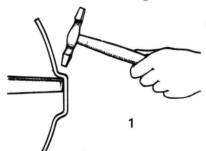

1

2

Diagrams 1 to 3 show stages in raising. Notice in each case the angle at which the raising hammer meets the metal to force it to take the shape of the stake. The metal must be held very firmly on the stake so that the shaping is accurate, if it is held too loosely the vibrations will cause hammer blows to be inaccurate and the shape to be distorted

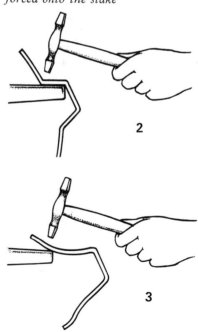

3

Modifying a shape

In addition to forming a basic shape by hollowing or raising, you can modify a shape by expanding or contracting it. You can open out or close in any part of the shape depending on the design.

The success of the operation depends on the stake you choose having a profile which is as close as possible to the finished shape you want to achieve. For flat sided shapes you can usually improvise with a selection of metal pipes or tubes of different diameters. For curved shapes you must have a round headed stake. The choice of hammer depends on the shape too. A collet hammer, a special hammer used for planishing (see page 118) is often used because the slight curve of its face makes it very versatile for this kind of work.

Sometimes it is possible to expand a shape by increased planishing over the area that needs to be stretched. An understanding of this technique is best gained by making plenty of practice pieces. Once you have come to understand the "feel" of metal beating and can regulate your hammer blows evenly and with a steady rhythm, you will learn where and when it is possible to modify the profile of a shape by this process. You should not use the modification process as a means of correcting mistakes, although it is often possible to improve a piece of work slightly, the modification should ideally have been included in your working drawing. You must be careful not to stretch the metal too thin or it may split. If the metal ever does split during any beating process, it should immediately be silver soldered and the work continued with great care. Anneal, pickle and clean the workpiece before starting on any modifications.

Seaming

Seaming is a process that combines techniques of sheet metalwork with silver soldering and beaten metalwork. First the metal piece is bent to shape, then the edges are butt-jointed and silver soldered together. The piece must be wired together for the silver soldering using a variation of the methods shown on page 80. After silver soldering, the workpiece can be raised upwards, curved, splayed outwards or planished. This is another silversmith's process and is especially suitable for making very tall vessels which can be cylindrical, conical, square, hexagonal or octagonal shaped. It is used for making things like napkin rings, candlesticks, coffee pots, jugs, vases and tankards. There are two methods for making a base. Either a separate piece can be cut out and soldered on, or the base can be raised inwards, curving until the opening becomes smaller and smaller. Close the tiny opening with a spot of silver solder. A base made in this way will need to have a ring base soldered on.

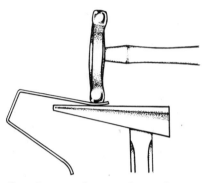

Opening out the top edge with a collet hammer on a funnel shaped stake

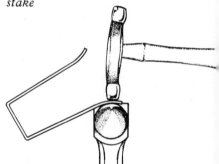

Opening out the top edge, this time working from the inside

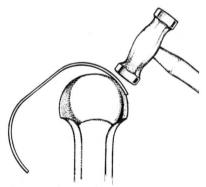

Contracting a shape on a curved stake using a flat faced hammer

Raising a bowl

Raising is not easy to learn. It is doubly hard to learn it from a book and if at all possible, you should try and get someone to teach you. If that is not possible, try and watch a craftsman at work. Here is the next best thing, a series of photographs showing in large, detailed close-up how a small bowl was raised from a flat blank.

The man shown working the metal is an apprentice silversmith of only six months' experience, working under the guidance of an experienced smith.

The object is to make a fairly steep sided bowl with a flat base measuring 2 to $2\frac{1}{2}$ in. (50 to 63 mm.) high. The material chosen is 12 SWG, about 10 B&S gauge (2.64 mm.), sterling silver, although any of the metals suggested on page 104 could be used.

To begin with, a circular blank $4\frac{1}{2}$ in. (114 mm.) diameter was cut from the annealed silver.

The work begins with a course of hollowing in a tree trunk former. Once the first simple curve is formed raising begins on a stake. After hollowing, a series of concentric circles, about $\frac{1}{2}$ in. (12 mm.) apart, are drawn on the outside of the blank and are re-drawn each time after annealing.

Above: The first round of hollowing is complete.
Right: Another couple of rounds have been completed. The edge is beginning to crinkle and must be smoothed out in the next course

A shallow bowl shape has been formed. You could stop here and move onto smoothing and planishing if you wished. The work has already been annealed once during the hollowing process. At this stage, once again the note of the hammer on the metal changes to a very distinctively duller sound indicating that the metal has work hardened. It must be annealed again to a dull cherry red then quenched in water before work can continue

Raising begins now, using a stake and a large raising hammer. You can just see faintly in the photograph one of the concentric pencil rings drawn on the metal as a guide to raising. Even the first course of raising steepens the sides of the bowl considerably. This is the reason why it is easier for an inexperienced worker to begin with hollowing instead of starting straight away on the stake

Towards the top of the first course of raising. The steepening of the sides has caused considerable crinkling around the top and great care is needed now to keep the shape and avoid bending any of the crinkles over into a fold. This photograph gives an indication of the amount of hard physical work involved in raising. The metal just ahead of the hammer head must literally be forced onto the stake and this means that you have to hit hard. The arm and hand holding the metal must exert great force too, as the metal must be held steady under the hammer

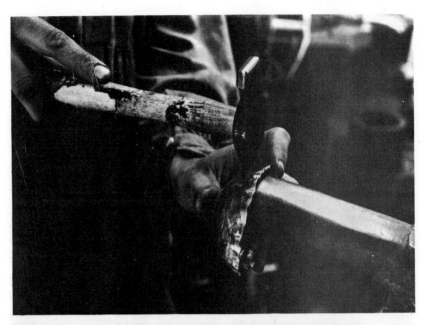

The final shape is almost there. You can see how carefully the smith has worked. The dents made by the hammer are quite regular and even. In this photograph too, you can see how small is the actual point of contact between the metal and the convex hammer face despite the large size of the hammer. The work has been annealed three times now since raising started.

The shape is complete and now the top edge is malleted smooth and flat with a heavy mallet. The next stage will be cleaning the metal then planishing and polishing

A finished bowl. You can just see the regular almost honeycomb shaped facets left on the surface after planishing. A pair of handles have been added to this bowl, although the basic shape could be modified in variety of ways, with handles of a different style, with legs, a base or even a lid

Planishing

Planishing is done after the shape has been formed either by raising, sinking or hollowing. The process consists of hammering the metal lightly and evenly all over against a curved stake to true up the shape and even out any irregularities and harden the metal. Planishing closes and refines the grain so that the metal will take a high polish. It leaves the surface of the metal covered with a series of small regular hammer marks in place of the irregular marks or ridges left by the shaping processes.

Planishing hammers and stakes vary according to the shape of the work. A planishing hammer is double faced. Both faces are highly polished, one end is flat, the other is circular and slightly curved. When selecting the hammer and stake, follow these general rules. Use the flat face of the hammer for planishing a curved surface and use the curved face for planishing a flat surface. The stake should have a slightly sharper curvature than the work. In this way, you only hit a small area of metal with each blow. The hammer and stake must be kept smooth and highly polished. This is the final hammering process and any flaw will be transferred to the metal with each blow.

Planishing conical and cylindrincal shapes requires a special hammer and stake because pieces of this shape are straight in one direction, curved in the other. The hammer is called a collet hammer. It has a rectangular face, straight in one direction, curved in the other. The stake should be similarly straight and curved. Improvise by using an iron bar, smooth and well polished, with the correct curvature and hold it in the vise.

Finishing processes

When planishing is complete, the top edge which will be uneven and irregular, must be trimmed and made true. Next, any base or handle or other attachment must be made, planished and soldered onto the body of the work. Each part must be planished individually before assembly. You cannot beat metal once the parts are joined as the hammering will cause distortion. Solder the parts together using either soft solder or silver solder as appropriate. Finally the work must be polished.

Truing the edge

Place the work on a flat surface and scribe around the top edge from a constant height as shown. Trim off the waste using curved snips and remove any remaining irregularities with a fine file. To give the edge a final smoothness, turn the vessel upside down and rub it on a sheet of fine abrasive paper which you have glued to a flat board.

Making a base

If you have made a bowl or dish with a rounded base by hollowing or raising then you will need to make some kind of base to rest it on. What this looks like depends on the design, but a ring base is

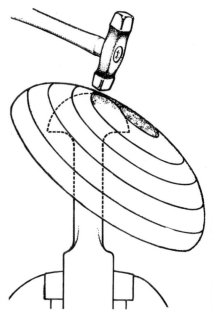

Planishing a bowl with a round headed stake. Concentric pencil lines act as a guide for the hammer

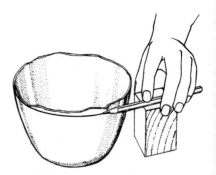

Truing up an edge after planishing. This wooden block and pencil method is quite easy to set up and easily adapted to any height. Hold the pencil still and turn the bowl, not the other way around

probably the most common and the easiest to make. There are two ways to do it.

Make a ring of metal and silver solder the joint together. Then you can soft solder the ring to the bowl. You can give the ring a slightly splayed base by hammering it over a stake along one edge. Be careful when hammering the soldered joint. If you hammer too hard you may crack the solder.

Alternatively, you can raise a wide, short cone shape from a round blank and cut out a hole in the center. Using this method you need only make one soldered joint to fix the ring to the bowl.

Shape the base ring with a file so that it fits the bowl exactly with no gaps. Anneal, pickle, clean and planish the ring using a length of pipe held in the vise as a stake. Trim off the edges, check the fit against the bowl and scour the edges on abrasive paper. Solder the parts together (see Chapter 5) finally removing any excess solder with an old file.

Hints on polishing planished metal

Polishing metal is explained in detail on page 122, however, when you polish planished metalwork remember that polishing will emphasize any faults, not hide them, so make sure that any scratches have been removed. The higher the polish, the more the flaws will be exaggerated. If you overpolish, you will loose the crisp finish you gave the metal by planishing.

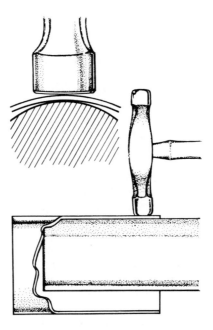

Planishing a cylinder. The straight sides on a shape like this will cause any irregularities to show up more than on a bowl shaped surface. Planish on a special stake or on a smooth pipe of the correct diameter. The inset diagram above shows the small area of the hammer face that actually strikes the metal

CHAPTER NINE
Finishing metal

Introduction
Once you have completed a project, there remains the pleasant and satisfying work of finishing the metal. The basic finishing processes like cleaning, smoothing and polishing the surface are common to most projects. Plain, polished metal is extremely attractive and this may be all the finish you require. Other finishes are dictated by the type of project and your personal taste.

This chapter is divided into two parts. First, the basic finishing processes required by all metalwork projects are explained in detail, this is followed by an explanation of a number of different protective finishes for many types of metal and for many purposes. The second part of the chapter provides a brief introduction to some decorative finishes which you can choose to give your work, and which you can add to you repertoire of metalworking techniques — etching, engraving and tooling for example.

Some of the decorative processes, etching and punching, for example, are easy and you can achieve successful results first time. Chasing, however, is a more complex and skilled process and enters the realm of jewelry and silversmithing techniques. Much of the information in this chapter is common to both jewelry and fine metalwork as well as the heavier techniques included in the rest of the book. Nearly all of the tools and implements mentioned here can be

bought from jewelers' suppliers.

CLEANING AND POLISHING METAL

The surface of a completed metalwork project must be made clean and smooth in preparation for the final polishing. Oxides, excess solder and any blemishes or scratches must be removed before you can start to polish.

A workpiece which has been annealed, soldered or subjected to any other form of heat treatment during working will need pickling in an acid bath to remove the oxides from its surface. The materials and procedure for pickling are explained in detail on page 106, be sure to follow instructions exactly as pickling can be dangerous.

The next step is to remove any excess solder from soldered joints with a file. Remember not to use a new file for this task, you will spoil the teeth needlessly. Needle files, if you have one or two old ones, will be very useful for cleaning up a soldered joint where larger files cannot reach.

Once the surface is clean it must be made smooth by carefully removing any nicks, pits, scratches or other blemishes which were either on the metal when you bought it or which were caused during the working process. For this you must use abrasives in varying degrees of coarseness, fine files, abrasive paper or cloth and finally polishing stone. They are

used in order, from coarse to very fine, until the blemish has been eradicated and the surface is smooth.

Files
Unless you need to remove quite large amounts of metal, use smooth and dead smooth files. Smooth files, skilfully used can give a very fine finish, especially if you use the drawfiling technique, explained on page 43.

Often, if you have worked carefully throughout the project, filing will not be necessary. Some workers remove large scratches with files before they start work.

Abrasive papers and cloths
Abrasive papers and cloths come in many grades from coarse to very fine. After you have used a smooth file, you will need a selection of the finer grades of abrasive papers and cloths. Make sure that each is marked with its grade number and that you always use them in order so that you are not undoing the work you have done. There is no difference between abrasive paper and abrasive cloth, except that the cloth is more flexible and will last longer. It can be bought in sheets or in a long strip wound into a reel. Crocus cloth is the name given to the finest of all abrasive cloths. It is used last of all for the final smoothing. It is not coated with an abrasive, but with red iron oxide.

Wrap abrasive cloth or paper around a wood or cork block for work on flat surfaces, and around a dowel or suitably shaped stick for contoured surfaces. A few drops of light oil on the surface will ease the work.

You can also use pumice as a medium to fine abrasive. Buy it either in powder form and apply it with a wet cloth or in solid form and dip it in water as you use it.

This stage of the work can be done by hand or you can use a grinding wheel or grinding attachment to a power drill. Use either the appropriate grade grinding wheel (see page 56) or you can cover a felt, canvas or cotton polishing wheel with adhesive and then with grains of the required grade. You can buy the abrasive grains from a jewelers' supplier. They are graded in varying degrees of fineness and coarseness, just like the grains already glued to abrasive papers and cloths. Pour the grains in a line on a sheet of paper, brush adhesive on the wheel and then roll the wheel in the abrasive. Leave it to dry for several hours. You must use a separate wheel for each grade of abrasive.

Polishing stone

Called Scotch stone in the United States and Water of Ayr stone in Britain, this is literally a very soft stone. It is used wet for the final smoothing and as it is softer than the metal, it wears away, leaving a muddy residue. Wash the residue off occasionally so you can check your progress. You can file the stone into any shape to reach into awkward contours.

How to smooth the metal

Always use files, abrasives and polishing stone in that order. Never skip from files to the stone. The object is always to move from a coarse finishing surface to a finer, and so remove the marks left by the previous abrasive.

It is impossible to say exactly which abrasive you should begin working with, you will have to judge for yourself, depending on the state of the metal. As a general rule, always start by using the coarsest grade that you think will remove most of the blemish. Sometimes you may not need to use a file at all. Remember though, to progress in succession from the coarsest grade required to the finest. Work with each one until you have removed the marks left by the previous grade. If you skip a step you will only be making more work for yourself.

The difficulty during this smoothing process is not to leave a depression in place of a blemish. Do not always work in the same direction across the metal, work across the blemish from all angles so as to remove some of the metal surrounding it and avoid creating a hollow.

All blemishes must be removed at this stage. Do not allow yourself to think that the next stage, the polishing, will remove flaws. Polishing only enhances faults, the higher the polish, the more the blemish marks stand out. So don't move on to polishing until all marks have been removed at this stage. If any remain, you must go back to the beginning and repeat the abrasive process until the metal is smooth and clear.

After smoothing, scrub the workpiece in hot water with detergent or soap to remove any abrasive dust and grease. Rinse and dry it thoroughly. The metal must be dry, otherwise any polishing compound which you use in the next stage will stick to the metal.

POLISHING

The purpose of polishing is to remove the fine marks left by the abrasive materials and the stone, leaving a gleaming, lustrous surface. There are very many kinds of polish, and particularly if you go to a jewelers' supplier you will find a bewildering array of different compounds of various kinds and grades.

The type of polish you use depends on the finish you require, the type of metal and the quality of the metal surface after you have finished smoothing it. You may be happy with the finish on your workpiece and only want to give it a final polish with one of the gentle commercial household metal polishes.

Rubbing the metal gently with very fine grade steel wool gives it a matt satin finish. You can achieve the same effect by using a wire brush on a grinding machine or on a horizontal power drill attachment. Wear goggles while you do this, as bits of wire can fly off. A matt satin finish, besides being attractive in itself, can sometimes be used to disguise a scratched surface, although bad scratches must be removed.

Polishes

Most jewelers' polishes are sold in solid form as a bar, consisting of a very fine abrasive embedded in wax. The polishes can also be bought in powder form for you to fix onto a buffing wheel with

adhesive. The bar form is easier to use. The only jewelers' polishes you will use for the projects in this book are tripoli and red rouge.

Tripoli removes the last marks of the fine abrasives and polishing stone, leaving a shiny unblemished finish. It is applied with either a felt cloth, felt jewelers' buffing stick or a cotton wheel on a grinding machine.

Rouge polishes to a brilliant mirror-like finish. It is applied with a chamois cloth, buffing stick or wheel. You can use these polishing compounds to polish hammers and stakes used in beaten metalwork too.

A selection of polishing materials. Clockwise: Sheets of emery paper with a roll of emery cloth and a polishing stone on top, a crimped brass wire brush, wool mop, stitched cloth mop, unstitched cloth mop, square bar of tripoli and bar of rouge.

Polishing by machine

Machine polishing disks come in many grades. Solid felt mops are stiff and hard and should be used as part of the smoothing process, where a lot of finishing is needed. Cotton mops consist of circles of cotton fabric held together in the center by fiber washers. The sections can be stitched together to make a stiffer mop. Wool and sheepskin mops are softer still, for the final polish. The wool mops can be used on their own, but the other disks are used with a polishing compound.

The polishing compound must first be put onto the wheel and then the workpiece held against the wheel. To put the compound on the wheel, turn on the wheel, hold the bar of compound against it until the wheel is coated. Use the compound sparingly. If you put too much on the wheel, the workpiece will be smeared with wax instead of being polished.

Ideally the polishing machine should operate at a speed of 1725 rpm. If the speed is in excess of 3450 rpm the metal will wear away too quickly.

Hold the workpiece against the moving wheel. Be sure that the wheel is rotating down toward you and that you are holding the workpiece below the central axis. In this way there is no danger of the workpiece being caught by the wheel and sent spinning dangerously. Hold the metal firmly, moving it back and forth. The abrasive action of the compound could cause small streaks, called "feathering," to appear on the surface of the metal. Rotate the metal constantly to prevent this from happening. It is wise to practice first on a scrap piece to get the feel of the machine.

When you move from one grade of polish to another, wash the workpiece in hot water and dry it after each application. Use a different wheel for each compound. Never put one compound on top of another on a polishing disk. Clean the disks after use with a fine bristled toothbrush and some household ammonia.

Always wear goggles to protect your eyes when polishing by machine.

Polishing by hand

If you don't have a machine, you can still achieve an excellent finish polishing metal by hand. If a piece has been made with care so that no unnecessary blemishes are formed during working and has been carefully smoothed, then hand polishing is a satisfying and not too arduous task.

To apply the polishing compound use either a tightly wadded piece of felt or chamois, or jewelers' hand buffs, which are simply wooden sticks covered with felt or chamois or lambswool. You can make your own hand buffs by gluing the appropriate material onto a stick of the right size and shape for your workpiece. Use felt with tripoli and chamois with rouge.

METAL FINISHES

Coloring metals

Metal is most often colored to emphasize highlights. The coloring darkens the metal which is then rubbed with fine steel wool to bring up the shine and the highlights.

Coloring is often done to darken copper or brass, to give the metal an antique effect. Jewelers often color silver pieces because the coloring is really a speeding up of the oxidation process which takes place naturally but much more slowly. Natural wear and use would keep the high spots shiny and free of oxide while the recessed areas would oxidize.

There are many different solutions which you can use to color metal, but the commonest one, used for coloring copper, brass and silver, is potassium sulphide, more often called liver of sulfur. It causes copper and brass to turn brown to black, and silver to turn bluish gray to black. You can buy it from a pharmacist or jewelers' supplier in crystal or liquid form. It smells unpleasantly of rotten eggs and must be stored in a dark container in a dark place as light causes it to deteriorate very quickly.

Directions for mixing the solution may be given on the label. Otherwise, dissolve a teaspoonful in a gallon (4.5 litres) of hot water. The metal must be completely finished and clean before coloring as grease affects the action of the chemical. You can either dip the workpiece into the solution using wooden tongs or you can wipe the metal with a rag dipped in the solution.

Watch the metal and when it has reached the color you want, remove it and rinse it thoroughly to stop the oxidation process. If you leave it too long, or if you have made the solution too strong, the oxide coating will become thick and will flake off in places. This is ugly and can spoil the appearance of the piece. If it happens you will have to remove all the oxide by pickling, then re-polish the metal before re-coloring it.

When the metal has been colored and rinsed, polish it very gently by hand using fine steel wool, to bring up the highlights. To preserve the highlights and colored shadows as they are, you can finish off with a coat of clear lacquer.

You can give brass a greenish antique finish by mixing 1 ounce (28 gm.) of ammonium chloride with 2 ounces (56 gm.) of salt and 6 pints (3 litres) of water. Treat the metal in the same way as for the previous method.

Coloring tin

Tin is oxidized with a solution of $3\frac{1}{2}$ ounces (100 gm.) of ferric chloride in half a pint (0.25 litres) of water. Brush the solution onto the metal. When it has dried, polish off the excess oxidation.

Coloring metals by heat

You can enhance the color of a metal with heat treatment. The metal should be clean and well polished before you begin. Heat it over the flame of a blowtorch, watching the change of colors carefully. Remove the metal from the heat as soon as the required color appears. Immediately quench the metal in water or oil. Remove the metal, dry it and rub it very gently with steel wool to bring out the highlights.

PROTECTIVE FINISHES

When you are planning what kind of finish to give a project you must consider whether the finished piece will need protection of any kind. Protective finishes fall into two categories—indoor finishes which are usually a means of preventing oxidation and keeping a shine, or outdoor finishes which must protect the metal against the weather and severe corrosion.

Lacquer
A coat of clear lacquer immediately after the final polishing preserves the shine on metal. After polishing, the metal must be made absolutely clean and grease free. Wipe it over with spirit or lacquer thinner or boil the metal in a washing soda solution. Dry the metal with a soft clean cloth. Do not touch it with your hands now or finger marks will show on the finished surface, use a cloth, tongs or wear gloves.

Warm the metal very gently in the oven to help the lacquer to flow easily over its surface. You can use spray or paint-on lacquer. For painting use a soft, good quality brush so as to leave no brush marks. Work in a draft and dust free room.

Paint
A coat of paint is usually given to iron and steel as a protection for outdoor use. Make sure there is no rust on the surface before you begin. Remove any traces of rust with a wire brush, files and abrasive paper. Apply a coat of primer paint before the top coat. For directions as to how to apply the paint and drying times, follow the manufacturer's instructions.

Wax
Waxing is a simple finish for indoor use. It is suitable for any metal. However, it is temporary and will wear off eventually, and then the piece must be re-polished and re-waxed. Warm the metal very slightly in the oven to make the waxing easier. Use beeswax or ordinary household furniture wax. Rub the metal briskly to a shine with a clean soft cloth.

Oil finish for ferrous metals
You can give ferrous metals a black rustproof finish with oil. You will need heavy lubricating oil or linseed oil. Make sure the metal is completely free of rust. Heat the cleaned metal slightly then rub the oil all over it with a cloth, giving a generous coating. Now heat the metal to about 300°F (149°C) for five to eight minutes, or until all the oil is burned off. This process causes a lot of smoke and an unpleasant smell, so do it outside if possible. When the oil is all burned off there will remain a slight oily film on the surface. As soon as the metal is cool enough to handle, rub it with a clean cloth to bring up a silky rustproof finish.

Bluing mild steel
Mild steel can be given a heat treatment, known as bluing, which protects it against rust. Clean and polish the metal first. Heat it to red heat then quench the piece immediately in oil.

Tinning
Tinning consists of covering a metal surface with a thin coating of tin, just like tinning in soft soldering (page 78). Copper eating utensils are tinned as a protection against the poisonous copper acetate or verdigris which forms as copper oxidizes. If an eating or drinking vessel is being tinned, then you must use only pure tin. You can use a soft solder with a high proportion of tin to achieve a decorative finish, but remember that solder contains lead, which is poisonous.

To tin a surface, first clean and polish it. Then brush it with flux. Hold the article over a low flame. If it is a hollow surface such as a bowl or dish, you can place small pieces of tin in it, if not hold the tin to the surface, rather as if you were holding a stick of solder to a joint or as if you were making a sweat soldered joint (see page 79). As the tin begins to melt, move the article around so that the tin flows evenly over the surface. Be sure to keep the metal at a constant heat while you do this. When the tin is evenly distributed, remove the article from the heat and immediately wipe the tinned surface over with a smooth clean cloth to complete the distribution of the tin. When the metal is cool, finish by rubbing the tinned surface with steel wool.

DECORATING METALS

Etching

Etching is quite an easy way of giving metal, particularly copper, brass and aluminum, an intricate decorative finish. There are basically two ways of etching. In the first and most traditional method, the whole of the metal surface is covered with a substance resistant to acid, such as varnish or beeswax, then the design is scratched in the resist to expose the metal. In the second method the design is painted on the metal with the resist varnish leaving the unpainted areas to be attacked by the acid. The piece is placed in an acid bath and the acid eats away the uncovered portions of the metal, leaving the protected areas raised above the etched parts.

When the resist is removed the design can be seen in relief.

Preparing the metal for etching

The project must be completed and all finishing and polishing done before etching begins. The whole surface of the metal must then be wiped over with spirit or benzine to remove all traces of grease. Grease acts as a resist and can spoil the etch. From now on, you must not touch the metal anywhere with your bare fingers. The greasy marks left by fingerprints are one of the commonest reasons for poor etching. Now the design and the resist must be applied to the metal.

Resists

Asphaltum varnish, known as Stopping Out varnish, made of asphaltum dissolved in benzine, is the commonest resist used for etching. For the traditional etching method cover the whole of the metal surface with varnish, not forgetting the back, sides and edges. Allow the varnish to dry, overnight, or for 4 to 8 hours. Don't leave it any longer than 24 hours as it becomes brittle and chips when you scratch into it making it impossible to etch a clear, clean line.

The metal must be hot if it is to be covered with a wax resist. An electric hot plate is the best way to heat the metal. Place the metal over the heat source and heat until it is uncomfortably hot to the touch. At this temperature the wax will form a beautifully smooth and even coating.

Transfer the design by placing a drawing or tracing over the varnished or waxed plate. Draw over the design with a pencil and you will leave a light but clear impression. To scratch the design in the metal use a scriber or a blunt needle pushed into the eraser on the end of a pencil. Remove large areas of resist by scratching with a craft knife.

For the second method, first transfer the design onto the metal with pencil or by using carbon paper. Then paint in the design with the varnish using a fine watercolor brush. Mistakes can be scratched away with a small knife, or wiped off with benzine. Scratches made on the uncovered area of the metal will be removed in the etching process. Be sure not to let any part of your hand touch the metal. If you paint in the design from top to bottom and rest your hand on a piece of paper or waste metal, this will not be difficult.

Unless you are etching inside a hollow vessel, both sides of the metal must be covered with resist. Pay particular attention to edges and corners, these areas should have two or three coats of resist.

Straight line designs can be etched using masking tape or adhesive plastic film as a resist. Cover the metal completely with the resist, again paying particular attention to edges and corners. Transfer the design to the resist, then with a sharp craft or utility knife, cut away the parts to be etched.

Preparing the acid

To etch copper, brass and pewter, use a solution of one part nitric acid to three parts water. To etch aluminum use a solution of one part hydrochloric acid to one part water. Mix the solution in a plastic, ceramic or glass container, large enough so that you can submerge the whole project. Remember the most important rule for mixing acid solutions—always add the acid to the water, *never* the other way around.

Etching the metal

The length of time the metal must

stay in the acid bath depends on the required depth of the etch. However, approximate times for different metals are as follows: Brass $1\frac{1}{2}$ hours, copper 1 hour, aluminium $\frac{1}{2}$ hour, pewter $\frac{1}{4}$ hour.

Brush away the bubbles that form on the metal with a feather, or stir the acid occasionally during the etch with a wooden stick. Do not leave the metal in the acid for too long, if you do the acid begins to attack the edges of the design and to eat its way under the resist.

When the etch is complete, remove the metal from the acid with wooden tongs and rinse it thoroughly in cold water. Remove the asphaltum resist with benzine or spirit and then polish the metal.

The acid gives off dangerous and unpleasant fumes during the etching, so if possible, do the etching outdoors or in a well ventilated area.

Mexican craftsmen make simple and attractive toys and household items out of tinplate using only simple tools. Use the things shown here to give you some ideas for small and easy projects. The pieces are decorated with simple punched and chased designs and can be joined with soft soldering and riveting

PUNCHING

Punched designs are stamped onto the metal with a special punching tool. The impression in the metal is the same as the design cut in the head of the punch. Punches are often sold in sets, for example, an alphabet or a set of flower designs. They can also be bought individually.

Punched designs are most effective if they are restrained. The project must be completely finished, cleaned and polished before you begin as no further work can take place once the punched design has been impressed on the metal, as you will risk distorting the punch marks.

Mark out the design and the position of each punch mark in pencil first. The metal beneath the punch should be well supported either by the bench top or by a block of hardwood.

The punch marks must all be of the same depth. Practice on a scrap piece of the same metal as that used for the project until you are able to judge the hammer blows accurately. Place the punch in position and strike it sharply once with a hammer. Never try and repeat a punch mark in the same place. The punch should not be hit so hard that the design is transferred to the other side of the metal.

Punching is such a simple way of decorating metal that much simple folk metalcraft, for example Mexican and early American tinwork, is decorated in this way.

A set of punches, each with a different flower design. Each punch is about 4 in. (100 mm.) long

Some typical flower and leaf
punch patterns.

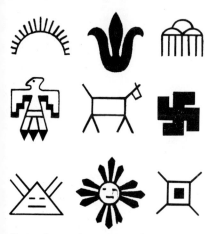

Sets of punches with traditional
Navajo Indian designs give a metal
project a completely different look
from flower punches. These
punches are usually used on silver
but of course, they can be used on
any metal.

Improvised punches

For simple decorations, you can improvise punches from things around the workshop. Center punches and dot punches can be used to make intricate dotted-patterns. An automatic center-punch would be suitable for this type of pattern because you can set it to punch to a fixed depth each time. In this way you can make patterns with dots of varying-depths.

You can make your own punches by grinding or filing the ends of large nails to different shapes.

Another example of Mexican craftsmanship is this attractive tin plate mirror frame. The flower petals are punched out and pushed up to stand in relief. The design has been highlighted with transparent colored varnish. Solder tabs on the back to hold the mirror and to hang up the frame

CHASING

Chasing is rather similar to punching, but the tools cut a patterned groove in the metal. This technique requires more skill than punching, but very intricate patterns can be made on the metal.

Chasing is sometimes confused with repoussé work as the repoussé hammer is used for both, however, chasing is done from the front of the work while repoussé is done from the reverse so that the pattern is in relief on the front of the metal. Repoussé is one of the most demanding skills of the silversmith, while chasing can be treated in a much simpler fashion, as it is here.

Chasing tools

There are two kinds of chasing tool. The tools used for outlining a design are called tracing tools, and the ones used for working the background texture are called matting tools. Silversmiths and jewelers, who do beautifully intricate chasing work have hundreds of tools at their disposal, each with a slightly different shape or matting pattern cut in the bottom, however amateurs need only a small selection of tools to make very varied designs.

The chasing hammer, also called a repoussé hammer, is a light-

A selection of typical matting patterns (far right), and (right) the ends of some tracing tools showing the shapes of the grooves they make in the metal

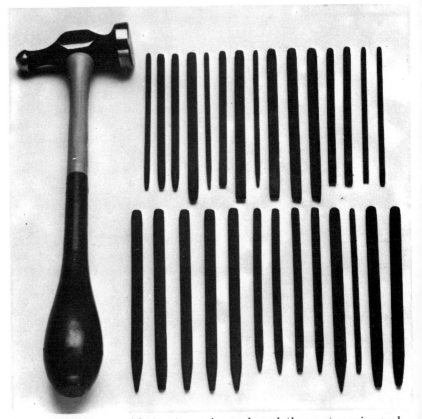

A repoussé hammer with (top) matting tools and (bottom) tracing tools

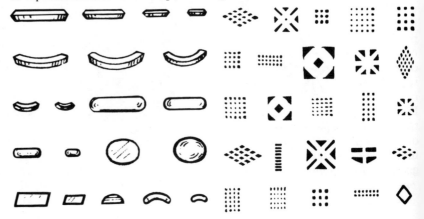

130

weight hammer with a broad flat face and a small pein. The unusual shape of the handle enables the hammer to sit easily and comfortably in the hand for the regular, repetitive blows of this work.

Chasing metal

The great skill in chasing is to hit the tool with exactly the required force with each and every hammer blow and also to hit the tool at exactly the right angle every time so that the tool moves through the metal but does not slip out of place.

The easiest metals to begin with are copper and brass. Skilled workers support the metal in a block of pitch which is solid but resiliant. You can use a hardwood or lead block. The metal must be securely clamped to the supporting base.

For a design where only low relief is required, you can pin the metal to a wooden board. This is one of the simplest methods of working, and would be ideal for a first attempt. Drive small nails or pins at regular intervals all around the edge of the metal. You will probably have to allow for the metal with the pin marks to be cut off afterwards unless there is some way of disguising it when making up the project.

Draw out the complete design on the metal in pencil. Begin by outlining the design with tracing tools and then texture the background with the matting tools.

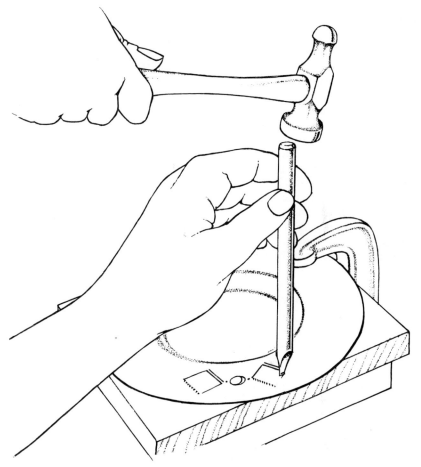

The correct way to hold the chasing tool and repoussé hammer. The project, here a plate rim, is held in a recessed block of wood so that the rim is supported all the way around

TOOLING

Tooling metal is very easy and is great fun to do. Thin metal foil is used and it is easy to work. The tools needed are simple, cheap and easily obtainable.

Suitable metals are copper, brass, bronze, pewter and aluminum. Aluminum can be bought in the required thickness in a variety of different colors. The metal should not be more than about 26 SWG and B&S gauge (approximately 0.4 mm.) thick. For most projects thicknesses of 32 to 36 on both gauges (0.27 to 0.12 mm.) are ideal.

For most tooled metal projects the thin metal must be mounted on a firm support such as wood or a thicker sheet of metal. Projects made in this way include plaques, boxes, mirror frames, lampbases etc. Tooling can also be used to make hanging projects like mobiles and Christmas tree ornaments, in which case no support is needed.

The tools are easy to find. You will need snips or scissors to cut the metal. For tooling the metal use wooden clay modeling tools with a variety of differently shaped ends. A dried up ball point pen and a stylus are useful too. The metal must be tooled while resting on a firm but resilient base. A hard rubber mat is best, although a pile of firm cardboard or newspaper can be used. A soft pencil, such as china marker or a grease pencil is useful for drawing on metal without making any impression.

How to do tooling

Work slowly and carefully, if you work too fast you risk thinning out the metal beyond its limit. Cut out the required amount of metal from the sheet, leaving an allowance all around for mounting the finished work. Draw the design on paper and attach the paper to the metal with tape or clips. Place the metal and paper on the work surface, and with a fine pointed tool, carefully and lightly trace around the design so that it leaves a faint impression on the metal. Remove the paper.

Now turn the metal face down on the work surface, and with a rounded tool, hollow out all the areas that will be raised on the final design. Work each area from the center to the edges, working with a circular motion. Try to keep the background flat. As soon as you have hollowed out all the areas, turn the metal face up and begin flattening out the background with a square ended tool. As part of the same process, you must also define the raised areas by outlining them with a pointed tool.

Turn the metal face down once again and repeat the hollowing process, increasing the depth of the hollows. Repeat the whole process of hollowing and then flattening and defining the background until you are satisfied with the work. Put in fine detail with a fine pointed tool, holding the metal over your hand and using this as a pad. The metal may need annealing during the working process.

When the tooling is complete, clean the metal if necessary in a pickle bath if it is very dirty and heavily oxidized, or with steel wool. The hollowed out areas on the back of the work must be filled to give support and to prevent the design from being dented. Use wax, rubber-based cement, wood filler, plaster or flour and water paste. Allow it to dry and then mount the work. Finish with a final polish and a coat of clear lacquer.

Tooling thin metal foil is not at all difficult and successful results are quickly achieved and look impressive

CHAPTER TEN
Projects

Planning your projects

Before you buy a piece of metal you should spend some time with pencil and paper planning exactly how a project will be made. Spend as much time as possible on this stage, thinking, sketching and reading basic instructions for the various techniques involved. Then go back to the beginning and double check your drawings and list of supplies.

Once you have settled on the basic design make a full size or accurate scale drawing of the project. It will be best if the drawing is full size as there will be less room for error when you transfer measurements. It is well worth buying a drawing pad large enough to take a full size drawing. Make the drawing as detailed as possible—include side views, top views and make a cutting plan for any flat sheet materials. Include as much information on the drawing as you can—the dimensions, the points where joins have to be made, shade in areas where one piece of metal overlaps another. For certain projects, particularly in sheet metal where a three-dimensional object has to be constructed from flat sheet, it is a very good idea to make a full size or scale model in thick paper or cardboard. In this way you can check the dimensions, the order and way in which joins and folds must be made as well as the overall design.

Once you have your design and scale drawing, you must think out exactly and in detail just how the pieces of metal you buy from your supplier are going to be turned into the project on the drawing board. Think about the metal—are you choosing the right one for the job? Are you choosing that particular metal because it is attractive or because it is tough, easy to work, or has special qualities, such as its ability to conduct heat? Have you chosen metal of the correct thickness—remember metal is sold by weight, so by cutting down on unnecessary thickness you not only save money, you also save yourself a lot of extra work as thick metal takes longer to cut, heat and drill. Is the thickness you have chosen going to be easy enough for you to work with the tools at your disposal, will the finished project be sturdy enough to fulfill its function?

Before you order your metal think whether the supplier can take any tedious work off your hands. Perhaps with his power cutting tools he can cut thick metal exactly to the size you require. He can make long cuts in sheet metal cleaner and more accurately with a heavy guillotine than you can with tin snips. It might be worth paying a little extra and ordering your metal in two or three pieces so that all the long or heavy cutting jobs are done for you and you only have to cut short lengths.

Think through every step involved in making the project. Read and re-read the instructions for the basic techniques involved. Write down each stage of the job as you think it through, and at the same time make a list of every tool you will need. Include in the tools list any extra bits and pieces you might need – if you read through the instructions for the simple projects which follow, you may be surprised to discover how many items are called for which are not strictly metalworking tools; things like drawing and tracing materials, paints, varnishes and brushes, fluids for cleaning brushes, rags for padding and wiping, oils, solvents, odd pieces of wood, some tools for shaping a wood form roughly for a particular job. Your work will proceed more smoothly if you have planned ahead and have all the items you will need on hand. Try and collect useful pieces of wood; you will find all sorts of small pieces a great help to act as supports, protection for clamps, shields for heat, packing, or for making simple jigs for all sorts of forming operations. Remember too, to include clamps, clips, tongs and other holding devices in your array of equipment.

Think about the order in which the work will be done. In what order should each cutting, folding and joining operation be made? It is very important that you think these stages through and so don't find yourself trapped in a dead end with two pieces that must be joined together but have been bent in such a way that the soldering iron, drill or rivet cannot get to the joint. Plan at what stage you should drill or punch the holes that will take the screws or rivets. This is one of the most difficult things to visualize, so make a scale model if you start getting confused. Think how the pieces will be joined—how easy will the joining method be for you to do? Will it serve its purpose—be functional, decorative, strong, waterproof? Will you need to buy any special tools to complete the job? Have you got drills or punches able to make holes of the right size for the screws, bolts and rivets you have selected—it will save money if you size these fittings to the tools you already have.

Does the project call for any special tools that you do not have. Can you borrow or improvise satisfactorily, or should you buy a new tool? What about any other accessories needed to complete the project—light fittings, wooden bases, hanging devices, stands, handles, bases, hinges. Will it be easier to buy things like this or can you make them yourself? Should you modify your project so that it can take a bought fitting. Should you form the metal around the fitting, in which case you must have the fitting before you begin work, or will you decide on the fitting once you have completed the work?

Consider the finishing methods at the early planning stages too. Will you have to pickle the finished project? If so, do you have a suitable container large enough? When the piece is constructed will you be able to reach all the outside surfaces with the necessary abrasives and polishes or should you

perhaps consider smoothing and polishing parts before you join them together? Will the finishing methods you have chosen for the metal be suitable for any fittings or accessories made from another material?

Decide whether you have chosen the right finishing method for the project—is it sufficiently functional, decorative, protective or will it involve you in a lot of extra work or in buying extra tools?

When you get your piece of metal home, always clean it before you start work on it and inspect it carefully so that the side which will be on the outside when the project is complete is the side that has the least amount of scratches to begin with. When working, try and protect the metal from getting any more marks or scratches. Keep the working surface clean and sweep away any filings or grit before you lay the metal down on the work surface for any operation.

On the following pages, detailed instructions are given for making five projects. All are simple and have been designed so that a beginner can tackle any one of them. Each one can be made with a minimum of tools and in a comparatively short time so that even on your first attempt you will be able to make something useful and handsome in metal.

Use these projects as springboard for your own designs. You can take an idea or part of an idea and adapt it to make something uniquely your own. For example,

any pattern could be etched into the border around the backgammon board, or you could etch your initials into the board. A chess board or other game board can be made in exactly the same way. The tooled metal bookends can be embellished with any design and you could use copper or brass instead of aluminum, or a larger base of decorative hardwood instead of plywood. The copper lantern could be riveted together instead of soldered. The design could be altered in many ways, the lantern given a pointed roof instead of a flat one, made round instead of square or given feet or a base to make it into a table lantern. Take the techniques used to make the brass and copper lampbase, but use rings instead of copper disks and you can make bowls, ashtrays and vases. Polish and smooth the insides with power driven, shaped abrasive heads which you can buy from a jewelers' supplier or hardware store to fit into a power drill.

The simplest project, the etched backgammon board, involves very litte work, but still requires that the metal be cut to size and that its surface be smoothed and polished. For your first metalwork project choose something like this that involves only one or two techniques and make each operation as simple as possible. You will then have begun to be pleasantly familiar with your materials and tools and will be confident and ready to move onto something more complex or elaborate.

Etched brass backgammon board

Materials
Piece of brass 0.4 in. (1.22 mm., 18 SWG, 18 B&S gauge) thick, 12 in. (305 mm.) square.
Tracing paper
Carbon paper
Fine paint brush
Scriber
Rule
Asphaltum varnish
Benzine or turpentine
A selection of fine abrasives and polishing materials
Commercial metal polish
Nitric acid, approximately 1 pint (0.5 liters)
Shallow plastic or glass tray large enough to contain the brass sheet.
Sheet of $\frac{3}{4}$in. (18 mm.) plywood or solid wood, 12 in. (305 mm.) square.
Adhesive
Clear varnish

First polish the brass with the metal polish and inspect both sides carefully in a good light. Choose the side with the least amount of scratches to be the face side. Remove any scratches and marks using the appropriate abrasives and polishing materials. The piece of brass used for this project arrived quite badly scratched in places and it required 150 grit abrasive paper as the coarsest abrasive. It was finished with fine abrasive paper, steel wool, tripoli and finally rouge applied with a lambswool polishing bonnet and power drill. Give the metal a final polish with the commercial metal polish, check that it is clear and smooth, wash and de-grease it.

Make a tracing of the complete design of the board and border. One quarter of the design is shown. Fold the tracing paper into four and trace each quarter in turn. Check that the points on the board alternate correctly. Cut the tracing paper exactly to the size of the board. Lay carbon paper over the metal and place the tracing on top, secure with adhesive tape. Transfer the border design only to the metal and draw in the line outlining the central area.

Remove the tracing and carbon, you will see the lines of the design reproduced faintly but clearly on the metal. Paint in the design with the varnish. Pay particular attention to the edges and corners of the brass. Then paint in the whole of the central area. Leave the varnish to dry for up to 12 hours, but not for so long that it becomes brittle.

When it is dry, place the tracing over the metal once again and go over the lines on the board with a ball point pen. Remove the tracing and you will see the lines impressed on the varnish. Etch the lines through the varnish with a scriber, using a rule to ensure that all the lines are straight.

Turn the brass over and varnish the back of it. Prop the sheet up on blocks of wood so that you can give the edges and corners another coat. Leave to dry thoroughly.

Etch the metal following the instructions given on page 126.

The piece shown here was etched in a solution of three parts water to one part acid for $1\frac{1}{2}$ hours. Rinse the metal thoroughly when you remove it from the acid, dry it and then remove the varnish with benzine or turpentine.

Prepare the wooden base, smoothing the edges and painting or staining them. Glue a piece of felt or leather to the underside of the base. Glue the brass to the wooden base following the glue manufacturer's instructions. Weight the sheet very heavily and leave the glue to dry. Give the brass a final thorough polish and degreasing then varnish the whole board with clear varnish.

One quarter of the complete design for the backgammon board.

138

Tooled aluminum bookends

Materials

Sheet of aluminum foil about 36 SWG and B & S gauge (0.1mm.) thick, large enough to cut two blanks each 14 in. by 10 in. (355 mm. by 250 mm.)
Tracing paper
Scissors
Wooden modeling tools, one with pointed end and one with flat end
Dry ball point pen
To mount the metal: 2 pieces of $\frac{3}{4}$ in. (18 mm.) plywood, 8 in. by $6\frac{1}{4}$ in. (200 mm. by 158 mm.)
2 pieces $\frac{1}{4}$ in. (6 mm.) plywood, 8 in. by $6\frac{1}{4}$ in. (200 mm. by 158 mm.)
2 pieces $\frac{1}{4}$ in. (6 mm.) plywood, $6\frac{1}{4}$ in. (158 mm.) square
$\frac{1}{2}$ in. (12 mm.) brads (panel pins)
Tack hammer
Paint or stain, clear varnish
Felt
Adhesive
Newspapers or rubber pad

Cut the aluminum foil to size with the scissors. Place one piece face down on the pad of newspapers. Trace the design and place the tracing on top of the foil. Secure with adhesive tape. Using the dry ball point pen go over the lines of the design very lightly so that they are lightly but clearly reproduced on the metal. Remove the tracing. With the pointed modeling tool, begin working over the design, indenting the metal and pushing it into the resilient newspaper pad.

Work from the center of the design outward along each branch

in turn. Irregular lines on the trunk and branches will give the appearance of bark, so you do not have to make the metal too smooth. The apples however, should be made as smooth and round as possible. Use the flat ended tool and work in a circular motion. Complete the tooling as explained in detail on page 132. Repeat the process for the other sheet of foil.

When you are satisfied with the design on both the pieces of metal, fill in the recesses on the back of the metal. Use a flexible filling material like wax or a rubber-based cement, rather than a brittle one like plaster. This is because the final mounting involves hammering and a brittle filling material would simply break up and shake loose.

To mount the metal and make up the bookends, cut the plywood pieces to size and sand them smooth, taking particular care on the edges. Paint or stain the edges and one face of the $\frac{1}{4}$ in. (6 mm.) pieces.

The metal foil is mounted over the $\frac{3}{4}$ in. (18 mm.) plywood. With a rule and set square, measure the size of the wooden block on the metal and make a tiny dot on the metal to indicate each corner and the center of each side. Lay the metal face down and place the wooden block over it, matching the dots to the edges of the wood.

Fold up the base of the metal, smoothing it carefully over the edges of the wood and making sharp clean bends. Secure it with a brad (panel pin). Fold up the two

sides and tuck the excess metal underneath to the base of the block so that it will be hidden completely when the bookend is made up. Fold over the metal at the top, folding the excess neatly across the sides and to the back.

Lay the mounted metal face down on a layer of soft cloth and nail the larger of the $\frac{1}{4}$ in. (6 mm.) plywood pieces to the back. To nail on the base, hold the block upside down in a vise, protecting the metal face with a padding of soft cloth. Touch up the edges of the wooden pieces if they need it and give the back and base a second coat of paint or stain. Finish the wood with a coat of clear varnish if required. Finally, glue a piece of felt to each base.

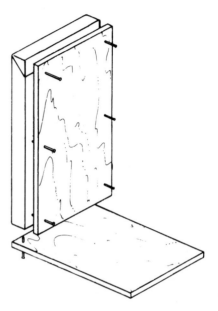

Fold the metal over the $\frac{3}{4}$ in. (18 mm.) plywood and then construct each bookend as shown

The complete design for the tooled aluminum bookends

Copper hanging lantern

Materials

Sheet of copper 0.018 in. (0.46 mm.) 26 SWG, 26 B&S gauge thick, 24 in. by 12 in. (610 mm. by 305 mm.)
Straight tinsnips
Small curved tinsnips
Scriber
Rule
Soft solder
Flux
Electric soldering iron
Pliers
Tongs
Wooden mallet
Drill with $\frac{1}{4}$ in. (6 mm.) bit
Center punch
Light fitting
Length of brass chain
1 in. (25 mm.) diameter brass ring
4 panes of glass, each 6 in. by 4 in. (150 mm. by 100 mm.)
Metal polish
Fine abrasive paper

Clean the metal sheet with the polish and inspect it carefully to determine which is the most unblemished side, use this as the outside.

With the rule and scriber, and the straight snips, mark and cut out the following pieces:

4 corner strips, each $1\frac{1}{2}$ in. (38 mm.) by $6\frac{1}{4}$ in. (158 mm.). Make a lengthwise right angle bend in each. 4 uprights each $\frac{1}{2}$ in. (12 mm.) wide by 7 in. (175 mm.). An extra $\frac{3}{4}$ in. (18 mm.) is allowed for on the end of each of these strips, this is bent up to provide a secure clip to hold each pane of glass in place.

4 horizontals, each $\frac{1}{2}$ in. (12 mm.) wide by $4\frac{1}{4}$ in. (108 mm.) long.
Base band, one strip 19 in. (480 mm.) long by $\frac{3}{4}$ in. (18 mm.) wide. Make four right angle bends at $4\frac{1}{2}$ in. (108 mm.) intervals, this leaves a 1 in. (25 mm.) overlap.
Roof, cut a $7\frac{1}{2}$ in. (190 mm.) square, and on the wrong side, scribe the cutting and folding lines and diagonals as shown in the diagram. Drill four holes as indicated to pass the chain through.

Take the light fitting and you will see that the fitting unscrews above the bulb fixture. The hole in the center of the roof should be the same diameter as the internal threaded portion of the light fitting so that the fitting will be secured in the lantern when its two parts are screwed together.

Place the internal threaded portion on the center of the roof blank and scribe around it. To cut out a hole this size, drill a series of holes on the waste side of the scribed line and finish off the hole with curved snips or a file. Cut away the waste at the four corners of the roof blank and bend up the sides.

The parts of the lantern are now ready to be soldered together. To help you fit them accurately, draw a side elevation of the lantern on your working surface like the one shown in the diagram. Remember to use a piece of waste wood as a working surface when soldering. You can then lay each piece in position on the drawing and keep it and its neighbors accurately in place while you solder.

Begin by soldering the horizontal strips to the central uprights. Now put two corner pieces in place on the drawing on the worksurface and solder one central cross piece to the corners. Repeat. Solder the remaining cross pieces to the corners to complete the four-sided framework. Check that the framework is square with the try square as shown on page 144.

Sweat solder the ends of the base band together and fit it over the framework. Check once again that all sides are square and solder it in place. Fit the roof over the frame and solder that in place.

The four panes of glass are slid into the lantern from the bottom and then the extra $\frac{3}{4}$ in. (18 mm.) on the upright strips is bent up and around the glass. However, the glass also needs something to hold it in place at the sides. Cut eight $\frac{3}{4}$ in. (18 mm.) long strips of copper and with the pliers bend each one into a square "S" shape as shown. Sweat solder each one to the inside of each corner piece at the position indicated in the diagram.

Pickle the lantern to remove the oxides caused by soldering (see page 106), or clean it with abrasives. Secure the light fitting and slide in the glass. Cut the length of chain into two equal pieces and thread each through two holes in the roof. Bring the four ends, together file or cut open a link in each end and bend them over the ring. The length of chain required depends on how long you want the lantern to hang.

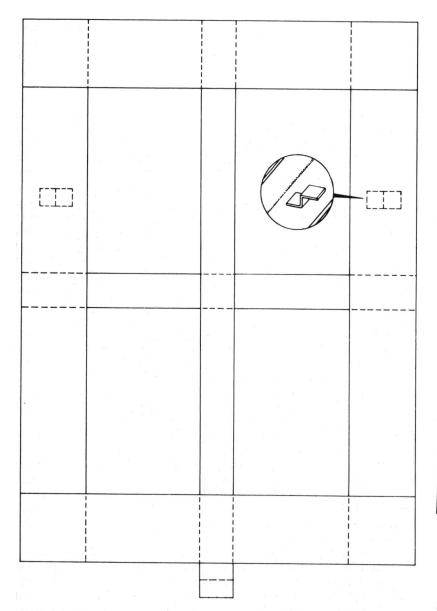

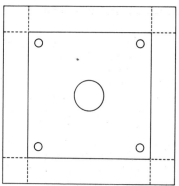

Diagram for the top of the lantern. Cut away the waste at the corners and drill holes as indicated

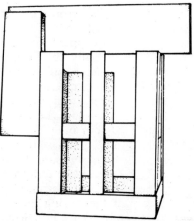

Full size side elevation of the lantern. The inset shows the positioning and shaping of the tabs to hold the glass in place

Use a try square at all stages to check that the lantern is being put together squarely

144

Lampbase in brass and copper

Materials
4 circular copper blanks, 3½ in. (89 mm.) diameter, ¼ in. (6 mm.) thick.
5 in. (125 mm.) of hollow brass tube, 3½ in. (89 mm.) diameter with walls ⅛ in. (3 mm.) thick.
Hacksaw
Try square
Power drill (ideally with vertical drill stand)
High speed steel drill bits
Abrafile
Soft solder
Flux
Large electric soldering iron
Blowtorch
Two 6 in. (150 mm.) C-clamps
Putty
Pickling solution
File
Polishing materials
Light fitting.

This is a very handsome project, but the materials can be quite expensive as the copper blanks may have to be specially cut to order from solid pieces of copper. However, the lampbase is not difficult to make and the final results are well worth the cost of materials and your time.

Check with a try square that the brass tube has a level base. If not, file or saw the base flat. Draw four rings around the brass tube at 1 in. (25 mm.) intervals using the method described on page 118. Secure the tube in the vise, or clamp it horizontally to the bench and with the hacksaw, cut it up so that you have four rings, each 1 in. (25 mm.) deep. Lubricate the saw blade as you work and make sure that you are cutting accurately on the line. Check that the sides and base of each ring are at right angles with the try square. File the top and bottom faces of each ring dead smooth.

Select the brass ring that will form the bottom of the lampbase and drill a hole through its side near the base. This will provide an outlet for the electric cord. Support the ring by clamping it over a large diameter piece of dowel or a piece of curved wood which you can shape roughly from waste wood. Use a lubricating fluid while drilling.

Drill a hole in the centers of three of the copper disks to allow the electric cord to pass through. A vertical drill stand will make this task very much easier than if you try and hold the drill yourself.

In the center of the fourth copper disk, the one which will form the top of the lampbase, you must drill a hole large enough to hold the light fitting securely and snugly. To do this, scribe a circle of the correct diameter then drill a series of holes close together all around the circle on the waste side of the scribed line. With the abrafile, saw through the thin pieces of metal linking the holes. With a file, smooth the sides of the hole until the light fitting just fits inside. There is no need to make the sides of the hole completely smooth, it will be hidden by the light fitting.

The lampbase is made by stacking up alternating layers of brass and copper on top of each other and then soldering the pieces together. The pieces are sweat soldered together, so first each of the mating faces must be tinned. Use the biggest electric soldering iron that you can find for this job as you will have to heat the solid rings and disks of metal right up to the melting point of the solder. The secret of success in sweat soldering is to have the faces meeting closely and also to have each tinned with the thinnest, smoothest layer of solder possible. Tinning and sweat soldering are explained on pages 78 and 79. To achieve a really fine smooth layer of solder, follow the soldering iron around with a rag, as shown in the diagram, wiping off the excess solder as the iron spreads the layer of molten solder over the metal.

Allow the pieces to cool, then reflux each face. Stack the pieces up, making sure that they are directly on top of one another. Clamp them together with scraps of waste wood under the clamps at top and bottom to prevent heat from being conducted along the clamps. Do not block off the holes drilled in the center of the disks; they are necessary to allow the escape of gasses released during the soldering operation. If you allow the holes to be blocked up, the gasses and expanding hot air will prevent the faces from ever meeting closely enough to be sweated together.

Construct a stable hearth for the soldering operation from firebricks, household bricks or stones. The drawing shows the improvised hearth rigged up from bricks which was used to complete this project. To sweat the pieces together, play the blowtorch over the whole metal stack. Keep the hottest part of the flame close to the metal and move it evenly up and down. Keep the flame moving fairly rapidly so that no part of the stack is without direct heat for long. It will take a good 20 to 30 minutes for the whole stack to reach sufficient heat to melt the solder. For this reason, make sure before you apply the heat that the metal is stable and secure and that you are comfortable and can reach all sides of the metal with the blowtorch without strain or discomfort.

You will see the solder bubbling at the edges of the joins when the correct temperature has been reached. Continue applying the heat until you can see solder bubbling on all sides of the stack. Remove the heat and allow the metal to cool thoroughly.

Before you immerse the metal in the pickle solution, plug the holes in the top and bottom copper disks with putty to prevent the pickle from getting inside the structure.

To smooth and polish the lampbase, hold it horizontally in the vise or clamp two thick pieces of wood on either side of it to hold it steady. An abrasive disk fitted in the power drill will make it very easy to smooth the sides, rub off any

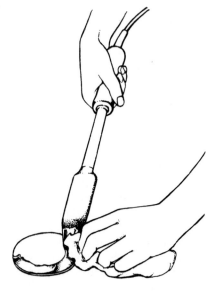

Tinning the edge of each copper ring and each brass disk. Use the largest soldering iron you can find and follow it round with a rag, wiping off the excess solder to get the thinnest possible layer

An improvised hearth rigged up from household bricks for sweat soldering the lampbase together

excess solder and remove the fire scale from the metal. Follow with fine abrasive papers and steel wool for a matt silken finish, or continue with tripoli and rouge polishing compounds for a bright shine. The finished lampbase will look as if it was made from three different metals because a thin silvery line of solder divides each layer of brass and copper.

Wrought iron bracket

Materials for one bracket

8 ft. (2.5 m.) mild steel strip, $\frac{1}{2}$ in. (12 mm.) wide, $\frac{3}{32}$-in. (2 mm.) thick
12 rivets, $\frac{1}{4}$ in. (6 mm.) long, $\frac{1}{8}$ in. (3 mm.) thick
Hacksaw or shearing tool
Scroll former
Punch or drill
Riveting tools
Primer paint for metal
Matt black paint for metal
Three screws
Paper
Pencil

This versatile wrought iron bracket can be used for a hanging plant, or with a second bracket, to support a shelf. The upturned end which serves as a hook to hold the plant basket will also keep a shelf in place.

First make a full size drawing of the bracket. Enlarge the tracing pattern, taking each square on the pattern to equal 1 in. (25 mm.) Keep the pattern by the bench as you work so that you can check the shape of the scrolls against the pattern as you form the metal.

For the frame, cut a 24 in. (610 mm.) length and make a right angle bend halfway along it. Then $\frac{1}{2}$ in. (12 mm.) from the end of one arm make another right angle bend to form the hook for suspending the plant. In the other arm make three holes, contersinking them if you wish, so the bracket can be screwed to a wall. Make a hole at each end and one in the center of the brac-

ket for the fixings.

For each of the two long scrolls, cut lengths of 17 in. (430 mm.). Begin curving the first scroll, working slowly and stopping frequently to check the formation of the shape against the drawing. Form the second scroll, checking it against the first, not against the drawing, so that you have a pair of matching scrolls.

Cut a 16 in. (406 mm.) length for the central double scroll. Curve the whole strip around into a semicircle and then scroll each end.

Lay the four shaped pieces of metal on the bench and fit them together, checking that each fits into place. Adjust if necessary. Cut an 18 in. (457 mm.) length of steel to form the straight strip inside the angle. Make a bend slightly less than a right angle, $\frac{1}{2}$ in. (12 mm.) from one end. Place the strip on the bench in its place among the other pieces and mark the point for the bend at the other end.

The pieces making up the bracket are now cut and shaped and should fit together easily without strain. The next stage is to punch or drill holes in the metal and then rivet the pieces together. There are two ways in which you can approach this stage. Either complete each joint and then move onto the next, or make all the holes first and then do all the riveting. If you follow the second method, fit all the pieces together after each hole has been made, check the fit, then mark the next hole. This method is slower than the first but is probably

less confusing for a beginner.

The general instructions for riveting (page 68) state that for accuracy all the holes for one joint must be made in one operation. However, in this case, as the pieces are curved, this may not be possible. To locate the holes accurately therefore, follow this procedure for each joint. Lay the metal pieces in position on the bench and draw a pencil line across the sides of two strips where they meet. Punch or drill the first hole. Put the metal piece back in place and make a pencil mark on the mating face by inserting the pencil point through the hole.

Join the pieces of the bracket together in this order. Join the two central scrolls together. Join them to the angle of the bracket and then to the ends of the arms. Join the double scroll at each end to the pair of scrolls. Join the straight piece at its center to the middle of the double scroll, then to the pair of scrolls on either side. Then join it to the angle at top and bottom.

If the bracket is to be used outside, give it a coat of rustproof metal primer paint. Paint the bracket with matt black metal paint for a traditional look, or use a paint of your choice. Mild steel rusts very easily so if you have any metal strip left over, check for rust then wipe it with an oily rag before storing it away until you want to use it .

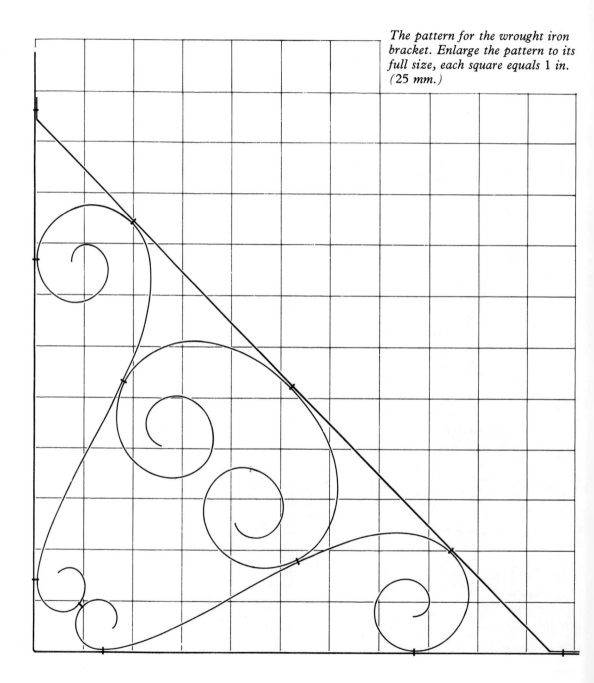

The pattern for the wrought iron bracket. Enlarge the pattern to its full size, each square equals 1 in. (25 mm.)

A variety of different wrought iron items made up of simple scrolls

Comparative tables

Standard Wire Gauge

Gauge	Inches	Millimeters
1	.300	7.62
2	.276	7.01
4	.232	5.89
6	.192	4.88
8	.160	4.06
10	.128	3.25
12	.104	2.64
14	.080	2.03
16	.064	1.63
18	.048	1.22
20	.036	.91
22	.028	.71
24	.022	.56
26	.018	.46
28	.015	.38
30	.0124	.31
32	.0108	.27
34	.0092	.23
36	.0076	.19

Brown and Sharpe Gauge

	Inches	Millimeters
1	.289	7.33
2	.257	6.52
4	.204	5.18
6	.162	4.11
8	.128	3.25
10	.101	2.56
12	.080	2.03
14	.064	1.62
16	.050	1.27
18	.040	1.01
20	.032	.81
22	.025	.63
24	.020	.50
26	.015	.38
28	.012	.30
30	.01	.25
32	.0079	.19
34	.006	.15
36	.005	.12

Inch fractions, inch decimals and millimeters

Fractions	Decimals	Millimeters
$\frac{1}{16}$	.062	1.59
$\frac{3}{32}$	.094	2.38
$\frac{1}{8}$	.125	3.17
$\frac{5}{32}$	.156	3.97
$\frac{3}{16}$	.187	4.76
$\frac{7}{32}$	.219	5.56
$\frac{1}{4}$	.250	6.35
$\frac{9}{32}$	.281	7.14
$\frac{5}{16}$	.312	7.94
$\frac{11}{32}$	.344	8.73
$\frac{3}{8}$	.375	9.52
$\frac{13}{32}$	.406	10.32
$\frac{7}{16}$	.438	11.11
$\frac{15}{32}$	.468	11.91
$\frac{1}{2}$	.500	12.70
$\frac{9}{16}$	.563	14.29
$\frac{5}{8}$	.625	15.87
$\frac{11}{16}$	.688	17.46
$\frac{3}{4}$	.750	19.05
$\frac{13}{16}$	.813	20.64
$\frac{7}{8}$	.875	22.22
$\frac{15}{16}$	.938	23.81
1	1.00	25.40

Comparative table of inches and millimeters

Inches	Millimeters
$1\frac{1}{4}$	32
$1\frac{1}{2}$	38
$1\frac{3}{4}$	45
2	50
$2\frac{1}{4}$	57
$2\frac{1}{2}$	63
$2\frac{3}{4}$	70
3	75
$3\frac{1}{4}$	82
$3\frac{1}{2}$	89
$3\frac{3}{4}$	95
4	100
$4\frac{1}{4}$	108
$4\frac{1}{2}$	114
$4\frac{3}{4}$	120
5	125
$5\frac{1}{4}$	133
$5\frac{1}{2}$	139
$5\frac{3}{4}$	145
6	150
$6\frac{1}{4}$	158
$6\frac{1}{2}$	165
$6\frac{3}{4}$	171
7	175
$7\frac{1}{4}$	184
$7\frac{1}{2}$	190
$7\frac{3}{4}$	196
8	200
$8\frac{1}{4}$	209
$8\frac{1}{2}$	215
$8\frac{3}{4}$	222
9	225
$9\frac{1}{4}$	234
$9\frac{1}{2}$	241
$9\frac{3}{4}$	247
10	254
$10\frac{1}{4}$	260
$10\frac{1}{2}$	266
$10\frac{3}{4}$	275

Inches	Millimeters	Inches	Millimeters	Inches	Millimeters
11	279	20¾	527	30½	774
11¼	285	21	533	30¾	781
11½	292	21¼	539	31	787
11¾	298	21½	546	31¼	793
12	305	21¾	552	31½	800
12¼	311	22	560	31¾	806
12½	317	22¼	565	32	812
12¾	323	22½	571	32¼	819
13	330	22¾	577	32½	825
13¼	336	23	584	32¾	831
13½	342	23¼	590	33	838
13¾	349	23½	596	33¼	844
14	355	23¾	603	33½	850
14¼	361	24	610	33¾	857
14½	368	24¼	615	34	863
14¾	374	24½	622	34¼	869
15	381	24¾	628	34½	876
15¼	387	25	635	34¾	882
15½	393	25¼	641	35	889
15¾	400	25½	647	35¼	895
16	406	25¾	654	35½	901
16¼	412	26	660	35¾	908
16½	419	26¼	666	36	915
16¾	425	26½	673	36¼	920
17	430	26¾	679	36½	927
17¼	438	27	685	36¾	933
17½	444	27¼	692	37	939
17¾	450	27½	698	37¼	946
18	457	27¾	704	37½	952
18¼	463	28	710	37¾	958
18½	469	28¼	717	38	965
18¾	476	28½	723	38¼	971
19	482	28¾	730	38½	977
19¼	488	29	736	38¾	984
19½	495	29¼	742	39	990
19¾	501	29½	749	39¼	996
20	508	29¾	755	39½	1003
20¼	514	30	760	39¾	1009
20½	520	30¼	768	40	1016

Index

Abrafile, 41
Abrasives, 120–121
Acme screw threads, 62
Adhesives, 73
Age hardening, 9
Alien key, 50
Allen screws, 64
Alloy steels, 13
Alpaca, 14
Aluminum, 8, 13, 14, 16, 92, 104
  to anneal, 61
  to drill, 45
  to solder, 74
Aluminum bronze, 14
Aluminum foil, 141
American National thread
  System, 62
American Standard gauge, see
  Brown and Sharpe gauge
Ammonium chloride, 124
Annealing, 9, 10, 61, 104, 111,
  113–115
Antifriction metal, see White
  metal
Anvil, 54
Automatic spring punch, 33, 129

Babbit metal, see White metal
Backgammon board, 138
Ball pein hammer, 52, 71
Beating down, see Sinking
Bench vise, see Vise
Bending fork, 96
Bending jig 96–97
Bending metal 85–87, 94–98,
  101–103
Bending spring, 100
Bicarbonate of soda, 106
Black mild steel, 12
Blind rivets, 72
Blocking hammer, 107
Blowtorch, 55
Bluing mild steel, 125

Bolts, 63
Borax, 80
Bossing mallet, 107, 109
Brass, 13, 16, 104
  to anneal 61
  to color, 124
  to cut, 41
  to drill, 45
  to etch 126, 138–140
  to file, 43
Brazing, 80
Bright drawn mild steel, 12
British Standard (Whitworth)
  thread system, 62
Bronze, 8, 14
Brown and Sharpe gauge, 18, 154
Buffers, polishing, 122–123
Buttress screw threads, 62
Buying metal, 16–19, 136

Calipers, 33
Carbon steel, 9
Carriage bolts, 64
Case hardening, 10
Casting, 9, 10
Cast iron, 9, 12
  to drill, 45
  to file, 43
Cast steel, 12
Center punch, 46
Chasing, 8, 130–131
Chisels, 25, 37–38
  to sharpen, 59
Chromium, 12, 13
Clamps, 36
Cleaning metal, 120
Collet hammer, 110, 112, 118
Coloring metal, 124
Combination pliers, 36
Combination square, 31
Conductivity, 9
Conversion tables, 19
Copper, 8, 9, 13, 16, 92, 104

  to anneal, 61
  to color, 124
  to etch, 126
  to solder, 74
  to tin, 125
Core diameter, 62
Countersink drill, 45
Countersunk screws, 63
Coursing, 111, 113
Creasing hammer, 82
Crest of a screw thread 62
Crocus cloth, 120
Cross cut chisel, 38
Cross filing, 43
Cross pein hammer, 52
Cut, of file, 42
Cutting block, 54
Cutting fluid, 45, 46, 66

Depth gauge 31
Diamond point chisel, 38
Dies, 67
Dividers, 32
Dot punch, 33
Drawfiling, 43
Drawing, 10
Dressing, a grinding wheel,
  51
Drilling 44–49
Drills, to store, 26
Drill gauge, 45
Drill stand, 49
Ductility, 9
Duralumin, 14, 92

Egyptians, 8
Endcutters, 36
Engineers square, 30
Etching 126–127, 138
Eye, to bend, 98
Extruding, 10

Ferric chloride, 124

Ferrous metals, 12
  to anneal, 61
Files, 42–43, 120
  to store, 26
File card, 43
Flat cold chisel, 37
Flat nose pliers, 36
Flux, 74–81
Folding bars, 82
Forging, 10

Galvanized iron, 13
Gauge, 18
German silver, see Nickel silver
Gilding metal, 14, 104
Gold, 8, 9, 15, 104
Goscut, 38
Greeks, 8
Grinding wheel, 56–57, 120–121, 123
Groover, 82, 91
Grooves, to cut, 41
Grub head screw, see Socket head screw
Gunmetal, 14

Hacksaw, 40
Half round chisel, 37
Hammers, 52
  ball pein, 52
  blocking, 107, 109
  collet, 110, 112, 118
  creasing, 82
  cross pein, 52
  hollowing, 106–108
  planishing, 118
  raising, 110
  repoussé, 130–131
  sledge, 52
  to store, 26
  straight pein, 52
  tucking, 82
Hand vise, 35

Hardening, 10, 60
Hard solder, 80–81
Hardie hole, 54
Heat treatment, 9, 60–61
High carbon steel, 12
High speed steel, 12
Hole saw, 47
Hollowing, 107, 113
Hollowing hammer 106–108
Hydrochloric acid, 78, 126

International Standards Organization (metric thread system), 62
Iron, 8, 12

Jewelers' suppliers, 16, 120, 137
Junior hacksaw, 41

Lacquer, 124–125
Lampbase, 147
Lantern, 144
Lead, 8, 9, 14
Lead, of a screw thread, 62
Leg vise, 35
Liver of sulphur, see Potassium sulphide
Low carbon steel, see Mild steel

Machine bolts, 63
Machine screws, 62
Magnesium, 8
Malleable casting, 12
Mallets, bossing, 107, 109
  raising, 110
  tinman's 110, 82
Manganese, 13
Matting tools, 130
Measuring systems, 18, 154
Medium carbon steel, 12
Melting points, 9
Mild steel, 12
  to drill, 45

Molybdenum, 8
Mops, for polishing, 122–123
Mushroom, on chisel 37, 59

Nickel, 8, 13, 15
Nickel silver, 14, 104
Nitric acid, 126
Normalizing, 10
Nuts, 63

Oil finish, 125
Outer diameter, of a screw thread, 62
Odd leg calipers, 33

Paint, 125
Pewter, 15, 104
  to etch, 126–127
Pewterers' solder, 77
Phillips screwdriver, 50
Phoenicians, 8
Phosphor bronze, 14
Pickling, 81, 104, 106, 124
Piercing saw, 41
Pilot hole, 46
Pinning, 43
Pipe bending machine, 100
Pitch, 62
Planishing, 104, 118
Planishing hammer, 118
Pliers, 36
Plumbers' solder, 77
Plumbers' suppliers, 16
Polishing, 120–123
  planished metal, 110
Polishing stone, 121
Pop rivets, see Blind rivets
Potassium sulphide, 124
Power drill, 48–49
Power grinder, 56
Pozidrive screwdriver, 50
Prick punch, see Dot punch
Properties of metals, 9

Protective finishes, 124
Pumice, 120
Punches, 33
  decorative, 128–129
  to sharpen, 58
Punch hole, 54

Raising, 110–117
Raising hammer, 110
Raising mallet, 110
Reamer, 47
Repoussé hammer, 130–131
Resist, 126
Rings, to form, 98
Riveting, 8, 68–72
  machine, 101, 103
Rivet set and snap, 70
Root, of a screw thread, 62
Rouge, 122
Roundnose pliers, 36
Rule, see Steel rule

Safe edge, 88
Safety, in the workshop, 29
Sandbag, 107
Saws, 40–41
  to store, 26
Scotch stone, see Polishing stone
Scrapers, 53
Screwdrivers, 50
  to sharpen, 58
  to store, 27
Screws, 62–64
Screw threads, to cut, 65–67
Scriber, 32
Scrolls, 96–97, 102, 151
Seaming, 112
Seams, on sheet metal, 90–91
Self tapping screws, 64
Set screws, 64
Setting out, 82, 84
Sharpening tools, 58–59
Shears, see Snips

Silver, 8, 9, 15, 16, 61, 104, 124
Silversmith, 104, 112, 113–117
Silver solder, 81
Sinking, 109
Sledge hammer, 52
Snips, 38
  to store, 26
Socket head screw, 64
Soft solder, 79
Soldering, 8, 9, 74–81, 144
Soldering irons,
  to store, 26
Soluble oil, 45
Spain, 8
Spanners, 51
Spelter, 80
Spinning, 11
Spirit of Salts, 106
Spirit level, 31
Stainless steel, 13
Stakes, for sheet metalwork, 82
  87–91
  for raising, 110–111, 114–117
  for planishing, 118–119
  to polish, 122
Standard Wire gauge, 18, 154
Steel, 12
  to drill, 44
  to harden, 60
  to temper, 60
Steel rule, 30
Storage space, 22
Straight pein hammer, 52
Studs, 64
Sulphuric acid, 106
Surface plate, 53
Swarf, 29, 44
Sweat soldering, 79, 148

Tapping, 65–67
Tempering, 11, 60
Template, 84
Tension file, see Abrafile

Terne plate, 13
Thread angle, 62
Thread cutting, see Tapping
Tin, 8, 15, 16
  to solder, 74
Tinmans' groover, 82, 91
Tinmans' mallet, 110, 82
Tinman's solder, 77
Tinning, 78, 125
Tinplate, 13
  to solder, 4, 76
Tinsnips, see Snips
Titanium, 8
Tooling, 132–133, 141–143
Toolmakers' clamps, 36
Tools, to buy, 25
  care of, 25
  closet, to make, 28
  racks, 27
  safety, 29
  to store, 26
Torque, 48
Tracing tools, 130
Tripoli, 122
Truing, an edge, 118
Tubes, to bend, 100
Tucking hammer, 82
Tungsten, 8, 9, 12, 13
Twist drill, 44–49
Twisting metal, 99

Unified screw threads, 62
United States Standard gauge, 18
Upsetting, 95

Vanadium, 8, 12
V-block and clamps, 36
Vise, 34

Washers, 64
Water of Ayr Stone, see
  Polishing stone
Wax, 125

Welding, 9, 11
Wheel dressers, 57
Whitworth thread system, see
  British Standard system
Wired edge, 89
Workbench, 23
  wooden, 23
  metal, 24
Work hardening, 9, 113
Workmate, 24
Wrenches, 51
  to store, 26
Wrought iron, 8, 12, 16, 150

Zinc, 15

Acknowledgements

Special thanks are due to the following individuals and companies who provided valuable assistance.

Fred Francis and Alf Martensson for help and advice throughout the progress of the book.

Paulo Lurati and Mario Cesari, silversmiths of Camden Lock, London for allowing us to take the sequence of photographs on pages 113 to 117

Buck & Ryan Ltd, London
E. Amette and Co. Ltd, London
H. S. Walsh and Sons Ltd, Beckenham, Kent, who provided tools and equipment for photography

J. Smith and Sons Ltd, Clerkenwell, London
J. and C. R. Wood (Metalcraft), Hull, Yorkshire
Black and Decker Ltd. who generously supplied the tools and equipment used in making the projects in the book

Photography
Richard Greenhill, page 6, 93
Ann Ronan Picture Library, page 83.
Macreadys Glynwed Distribution Ltd, page 17